Schtick

"These are the poems, people."

kevin coval

 Haymarket Books
Chicago, Illinois

Copyright © 2013 Kevin Coval

Published in 2013 by Haymarket Books
PO Box 180165
Chicago, IL 60618
773-583-7884
info@haymarketbooks.org
www.haymarketbooks.org

Trade distribution:
In the US, Consortium Book Sales and Distribution, www.cbsd.com
In Canada, Publishers Group Canada, www.pgcbooks.ca
In the UK, Turnaround Publisher Services, www.turnaround-uk.com
In Australia, Palgrave Macmillan, www.palgravemacmillan.com.au
All other countries, Publishers Group Worldwide, www.pgw.com

ISBN: 978-1-60846-270-4

Cover design by Brett Neiman.

Published with the generous support of Lannan Foundation and the Wallace
Global Fund.

Printed in the Canada by union labor.

Library of Congress Cataloging-in-Publication data is available.

10 9 8 7 6 5 4 3 2 1

Praise for Kevin Coval and *L-vis Lives!*

"One of my favorite poets."
—**Mos Def**

"Kevin Coval is a new, glowing voice in the world of literature." —**Studs Terkel**

"*L-vis Lives!* is a cultural touchstone, a book that will easily move into a space that's been waiting for much too long."
—**Patricia Smith, author, *Blood Dazzler*, finalist for the National Book Award**

"[*L-vis Lives!*] is bold, brave, and morally messy—twelve rounds of knock-down, drag-out shadowboxing against a shapeshifter. The dark humor, intellectual fervor, and emotional rigor Coval brings to bear animates these pieces, turns caricatures to characters, implicates us all. It's about time."
—**Adam Mansbach, author, *Go the F**k to Sleep***

"A radically candid collection . . . daring, historically grounded, and socially cathartic poems. . . . Coval's air-clearing honesty about violent and insidious racism and authenticity and creativity is blazing and liberating."
—**Donna Seaman, for American Library Association's *Booklist* magazine**

"A prophet . . . a tour-de-force . . . he can soothe and scathe, hurt and heal, in the course of a single poem."
—***Providence Journal***

"Coval's greatest strength is his rhythmic, beautiful prose and his willingness to speak truth to power, no matter what the personal cost."
—***URB***

"A conscious Jewish phenomenon . . . [Coval's] work speaks to the Jewish relationship to the American color line."
—*Jew School*

"This book reminds me that if anyone can change the world, it will be the artists and the poets."
—**Henry Chalfant, producer, *Style Wars***

"As insane as it may seem, much writing about hip-hop, especially about white kids and hip-hop, eschews the discussion of race or racism. *L-vis Lives!* honestly, beautifully, and emotionally illustrates the contours of that discussion. And it reads like heavily syruped pancakes."
—**Boots Riley of The Coup**

"Coval brings artistic taboos to light."
—**Rhymefest**

Table of Contents

tuesdays with mel gibson

the secret relationship between Blacks & jews

all the pharoahs must fall

post-schtick

for Joyce Sloane
the Mother of Chicago
theater, the Second City & Borscht Capades
my G-dmother & #1 Aunt.
i miss u every day

"Going to war with the melting pot . . ."
Raekwon the Chef, Wu-Tang Clan

schtick: an arse poetica

my father abraham
is not my father
Danny
not my father
James Baldwin
KRS-ONE
certainly not
my father
israel.

israel is not my father
unless my father is
abraham. i am
isaac. i am
isaac means we are
sacrificed by some
demented call.
the i is
we, israel
some white/lamb
some whiteland/america
is abraham to israel's
isaac, some whiteman.

this is assimilation
schtick, see
nothing rhymes
with Palestine.
nothing in hebrew
nothing in yiddish
nothing in a state's diction-
ary.

whitemen can't rhyme
can't sing. whitemen
dictate. eat dictator chips
whitemen selfish shellfish
sell fishy democracies.
oh say, can jew
amer-u-can
with your
toucan

this is shit
schtick. a laugh
a gas. a laugh
at the gassed

guess what
herring but

this is assimilation
schtick. my father is schtick
shit see the arrange/ment
derange-ment of letters
too close. columbus/colonial
democracy/fallacy
philistine/Falastin
Palestine-berg

see what i did
father
land
the en/d-
ing?

א aleph א

kike (kīk) *n.* (pl. *kikes*) [Yiddish *kikel*] 1. ellis island, christian papers stamped cross. dark-mustached italian bureaucrats in high blue felt hats black rubber branded us a circle; *kikel*—we whispered and some dumb mickwopcrackerpolack shortened it like our last name: kike! 2. enclaves, huddled in a stranger's land, rounded synagogue windows; knelt before kings who let us earn a living while we speak to Ours in secret tongues. 3. kikes of zion, dirty money diamond lenders; hollywood vegas masonic blueprints. 4. scapegoat, paschal lamb, isaac/ishmael—blamed for plagues on pharaoh. 5. cossacks killed kikes like the spanish romans christians germans italians french russians american roosevelts turning backs and boats around—christians christians christians. 6. ethiopia, africa, egypt moses black manna orphaned rivers. 7. rounded in boxcar lines awaiting deportation extermination salvation from christ-killing revisionists. 8. families broken—names changed, converted nose job cul-de-sacs. 9. kabbalah madonna idolatry. 10. gelt in our socks hidden like pe'at and sliced cocks, yarmulkes beneath fresh shtetl lids; assimilateable. 11. kikes are (not) white 12. full circles, history gorging its tail 13. kikes are (not) white—*quit your colonialism!* 14. building walled jerusalems, closed knesset theocracies. 15. kikes are (not) white. 16. never again—cycles recycle, can't say we didn't see it coming. 17. remember the covenant. 18. come depression: start running.

after A. Van Jordan

trans(atlantic)lation

these are the tongues in my mouth:
a barrel of pickles
a pool of cod
my father the storyteller
gags, george burns's jokes, broadway
the year overseas: an english
of mutton stew, fish & chips and curry
of course Chicago
and which side
its borders, my own diaspora
pilsen four years
Gwendolyn Brooks, Algren's
northside polish haunts
the stark light of day
break in an alley. a walk-
a-bout of historic mounds
wounds i have songs for
closed and shut down. spots
disappeared. the pidgin
of the academy i learned in public
libraries. a post-modernity
for post-industrialism. journals
and books on hold. the Sulzer
my preferred branch
ransacked for blues
this city has born.
there is the crutch
of suburbia, the *likes* and *ya knows*
i've tried to excavate
the north shore nonchalance
the world customized for you.

there are students who stack my vocabulary
with the latest ingenuity. south- and westside
joes who pledge allegiance to southern rappers
who sound like where their great grandma came from
vowels slow roasted like bbq words on a spit
in your mouth, yes y'aawwwlll.
there is the synthesis of this. the blend
of Flash's hands, mixed strands on the tongue.
the sense of the sentence, its regionalism
and broken syntax.

my family cannot feel me
fully. i speak a fractured tongue.
a new yiddish, an english of broken
worlds, new words mashed together.
an appropriate appropriator. maybe
the network will get the message
i scribble in bottles of old english.
Rog & Idris, Angel & Denizen
anyone mixed and working and torn
between two cultures or more
bridged between multiple devotions
practiced in Wu-Tang slang, X-clan science
the specificity of woody allen neurosis
the outrage of stones vs. tanks
anger and diction. the desire
to communicate, to be felt
for real
for real
& (w)holy

chosen

check the books, the bones, the house
of jacob chose not to chew on cud.
it's a good look. in the desert
beneath the endless canopy of sky
we chose one, out of all indigenous
offerings and adorning, all particular forms
of fire and water worship, of all G-d's dirt
and gold we chose to call it all   the same
sacred/profane. unify the two
in the same mind. same time. all
beneath the endless canopy of sky, one
singular sensation, one giant flame, sacred/profane
all back from and back to Ayin-
(yang). again, not just justice
for just jewish vagina, all vagina.
the messiah will come from Ruth's
tribe, a moab convert. to choose
one is a conversion, a great reckoning.
one unknowable, one un-nameable
one humane, one horrible. a con's
version of the Giant story. we david
we psalm. we chose the scared
sacred out of our diasporic minds
running again, Ayin, in the desert
there must be some common
denominator, some common man
some *nom de plume*, some math
in the ghost face of all this running
all this reckoning, a common name
beneath the canopy of the infinite
the imagined and unknown expanding

universe, all peoples and petals in distant
lands, all tribes of different tongues
and scarification rituals, all the worships
and warships, everywhere beyond here
and everything here and hillside and across
the wall of the infinite, border and burden
we call it the same   name
Adonai
beneath the endless canopy of sky
we name it all, All
we chose to call it all, All
All   One

mezuzah

one on the inner door of the apartment at 1750 West Haddon
an Irish neighborhood where George lurked late
after taking Pearl all the way
south to her Polish block at 17ᵗʰ and Kostner.

one on the suburban sprawled Skokie bungalow
where Sy and Ellie fought in front of my mother
where she watched hers perfect the affect-ed smile
fraud, porcelain and glass jaw.

one in the ghetto in Venice
where curved doorways marked temples
like a secret language they hoped wasn't
cracked by Mussolini guards and neighbors.

one craved in the wooden doorway of the Sabbath
house where I ate in India, where the hosts spoke Hindi
and English, served dal and roti, and got mad
pissed cuz i didn't know Hebrew.

one in the mikvah in Montreal where naked I washed
my sins, which are multiple and egregious and forgiven
by Hashem if I admit them before Yom Kippur in this minyan
of Hasids who swing chickens overhead and hawk diamonds.

one in the shul in Cape Town where diamonds are white
and oil is black and during apartheid the congregation
iced in silence, learned the rand will carry you like a stork
from the bloody mess of otherness to (re)birth you: colonial and clean.

one at 95ᵗʰ and Riverside, in a two-bedroom near the Hudson

where my G-dfather puts his two children to sleep, pours a drink and burns oil through the night to write side-project stories and poems about the city he loves. Central Park his Zion.

one nailed to the back entrance of the North Carolinian home I visited the family of the only jewish girl I've dated and was supposed to marry whose seder had sweet potatoes, sweet tea and tzimmes, whose Hebrew was biblical and Zadie all Brooklyn. i fled, cowardly, in the middle of night.

one on the eighth floor at 3800 Lake Shore Drive, facing Jerusalem and Mecca where my #1 aunt Joyce Sloane rose with the sun over Lake Michigan to mother all comedy in the Second City. her back room a halfway house for addicts, drunks, and valiant Hollywood efforts; room to me, for over a year.

one around my neck, silver and flat, a gift from my mother, resting on my chest which is hairy and heavy with hope to be a good son, a good jew and brother, a good writer and teacher, a mensch in the new mil-lennium, to allow YHWH to enter my heart open its door to revelation and prophecy, to prostrate in my body, the temple.

midrash of the body

after Jeff Kass

beneath my yarmulke
horns. benny good-
man of the skullcap.
beneath the horns
a fallen angel, a christian
revision to fare well
in front of roman governors.
beneath rome, bodies
piled like corned beef
at Manny's Delicatessen
roadside graves
in a german countryside.
beneath a german is a chicken
heart, a tin swill of pissy lager.
pregame and afterparty
during recession, a flock of lambs.
beneath recession a choir
of banks, acronymed world orgs
that don't need a conspiracy
theory. elders of zion
balding at the heads
of tables before microphones
explaining to congress why
billionaires are bailed out
first. all the suits complicit.
beneath them are tailors
and pawn shop capitalists
bearded men with a sock
of rubles, rubble, a net worth

that is a network of cousins
who have an uncle a town over.
the world is over and can be
made again. beneath the rubble
isaac's swapped body, a scapegoat.
a pyramid scheme built and sold
down the nile. against stream
like salmon, a bagel with schmear
the queer, the world   over
and can be made again
the world is over and can be made
again. my body Isaac, my body Ishmael
we need to go   to go
on the lamb.

semite

the semantic
branch of semiotics.
this is how we use it
montell jordan, pragmatics.
from the hebrew *shem*
meaning name. the pseudo
shems we smite by, go figure
or reconfigure. *X* the unclean
the unknown, the variable
and verifiable. the varied
semites are an afro-asiatic
people, polyglot-erus
arabic and aramaic, before
jesus and jewish. phoenicians
gypsies and egyptians. fleeing
them. settling with semites
in Palestine, all the descendents
of Shem, Noah's son, *a black man*
in Africa. if you repeat this fact
they can't laugh atcha[ℵ] can't call
you anti-semitic for saying
the protocols are segregationist
they wall and patrol semites
with semiautomatic weapons
in the name of

[ℵ] KRS-ONE, "Why Is That?"

benℵ

ben Da-vid Yosef
my father in hebrew.
in english, Danny:
Danny's Place
Danny's Dogwalkers
ben invention, american
capitalism. its demands
to scrape. ben scraps
ben droppings other
men leave: tips, shit
in a plastic bag. a country
no one wants in the first place.
ben movers and shake
downs. ben shade: esta ft.
lauderdale, oslo. ben civil rights
fractures. ben ascendance
into white-ness. ben skin
privilege and passing. ben
nation state. ben/t borders
past tense. ben borders
and birthright. circumcised
sons on set/tled land. foreskin
four hymns sung by the youngest.
ben country clubs with restricted
membership. ben divorce
broken ketubahs. broken glass
everywhere. kristallnacht
in the strip mall. kristallnacht
in the Gaza Strip. ben doctors

ℵ Means *son* or *son of* in Hebrew.

who refuse health care. ben
bankers who disallow self-
determination. ben jews
on beaches. the sun only
for ben passports. other
sons unable to pass ports
while supplies demanded
Mavi Marmara, flotilla. ben
killers. ben raiders of lost art:
finesse and compromise
communism, communalism
ben fathers who were
pushed around themselves.
ben the bullied begat sons
who bully. ben a bitch.
ben sarah / barren.

the family business

"this is for the family that can't be with us"
Kanye West, "Family Business"

the singer of songs

my father is a tzaddik.
a tzaddik is a righteous man.
my father is a tzaddik
not a saint. saint is a christian
word. we are not christian.
we are jews. my father
is a tzaddik. a first generation
American tzaddik born here
of circumstance. the broad
shoulders of Chicago housed
his parents from Aryans. Edgewater
held his first dreams, post-Shoah
dreams of American idealism
a civil-rights baby who saw Ernie
Banks as the city's Martin King
and knew whoever wouldn't afford
Mr. Cub the same rights as J. Daley
must be meshuggah. a city
he would never leave 'cuz it needs
that kind of care, it's that kind of town
Chicago is . . . home to my father
a tzaddik, a righteous man, he is, he is
a cantor. he sings to me all the songs.
all the songs he sings to me, all the songs
of history. he is a cantor. a righteous
cantor, he sings to me the songs of our history.
on an empty field in Fox Lake, playing catch
the wind was blowing a song. my father sang
the trials of Hammerin' Hank Aaron, his death
threats chasing records. he said Willie Mays
went into Leo Durocher's office as a rookie struggling

to get on base and told Mr. Durocher, *i'm not sure if i can
hit major league pitching* and my father said Mr. Durocher said
Willie, you are my center fielder, get out there and play
and G-d has told that to my father
and my father has sung that to me 'cuz
he is a cantor, a righteous cantor
a tzaddik, the singer of songs.

on becoming a man

the day of my bar mitzvah felt no different
than any other february day in Chicago.
i woke cold

with a boner thinking of Melissa Brown
a shiksa with a pool table in her basement
whose parents never seemed to be home.

the synagogue was packed with cousins
i never met, friends my dad once did business with
or might have to borrow money from.

before the service began the rabbi and i talked
in a room to the side of the bema.
he made me promise

i would not return to be confirmed.
this would be my last day as a member of the congregation.
my mom owed too much in unpaid tutoring fees.

i was thirteen and restless and knew
the rabbi was racist 'cuz when i told him
Moses was Black, he said that was impossible.

my haftorah was memorized and meaningless.
who thought to make boys the center of a room
with ripe acne, underarms, a million dick jokes

what makes us men?

the reception was awful. my parents, divorced four years

in the same room under court order. too many wrinkly-breasted women
trying to put their clown-lipsticked mouths on my face. the fucking
DJ was a glam-rock feathered-mullet d-bag who played mötley crüe
instead of the beastie boys. i'm a real brat, a jewish american prince.
i got an armful of happy bar-mitzvah hallmark cards stuffed with $50
war bonds. in four years, the money would be repossessed, my family
on a carousel of bankruptcies and interventions. it was '88, a moment
of big-haired suburban reaganites with coke in their purses and the
beginning of hip-hop's golden era. the dual–tape deck boom box at the
foot of the bunk bed i shared with my little brother, an escape window
i'd climb thru.

what is this cult of manhood?

on the night of my bar mitzvah
Melissa Brown let me touch
what bloomed beneath her shirt.

i felt like a boy
awed and unsure.

i am a man
awed and uninsured

on the broke side of the constant war
against the working.

twenty-some years removed

my minyan, a tribe of poets
unkosher and holy
profane and prophetic.

they speak the new language.
it enrages the rabbis

but this is what men do:

tend the fire
survive the wilderness.

schtick (at eric's bar mitzvah)

after watching the VHS tape my mom converted to DVD

the party was held at a BBQ, wild west–themed chain restaurant. i am
not sure who decides these things, to dress jews living twenty minutes
outside of Chicago in straw hats like cowgoys. my brother, big-headed
and buck-toothed, wore a red bandana around his neck. no jesse james
or crip killer. he looked like tweety bird impersonating Tupac.

mostly jewish kids at the party, with the exception of the tiny seventh-
grade blonde girl my brother selected for his first dance. the bar mitz-
vah: an initiation into adult shame and humiliation. the shiksa my
brother selected to dance was not a happy camper. once their small
bodies met at the waist, her head tucked behind his ear in slow jam,
her eyes rolled into the top of her head, the OMG totally-as-if white girl
equivalent to the black woman's disgust and tooth suck, the frat boy's
no fuckin' way, bro, the blues man's *shiiiiiiiiiiiiieeeeeeeeeetttt*!

all this would never really have been known or remembered until
mom put it on DVD, gave it to Eric as some sort of sadistic present,
now enjoyable for all eternity in slow-mo rewind, especially when the
dishwater barbie dodges his kiss as the perm-rocking, coked-out shitty-
ass bar-mitzvah circuit DJ aka mr. failed musician with pedophilic ten-
dencies says creepily into the acoustic mess of the microphone,
champagne snowball . . . and my brother keeps leaning to plant a root-
less smooch on the overly perfumed air where a freckled cheek has re-
cently departed.

but the real treat, aside from the big hair, shoulder pads, jewfros and
gaudy, gigantic sweaters in the chow line (and the two-step dance com-
petition won by an old, drunk couple no one in the family remembers
inviting) was the speech ceremony given by my brother's male elders,

24

his jewish role models who welcomed him to the minyan on this day of pulled pork sandwiches, Jim Beam shots, and stare-down-gun-draws-this-town-ain't-big-enough-for-the-both-of-us-type-looks launched across tabletops between divorced sides of the family.

my father went first. the dance floor cleared. my brother sat in a foldout chair stage right, the DJ turned down Rick Astley but left the red ambulance lights still swirling to introduce Eric's dad with a little pizzazz. my dad was skinny then. glass frames from top lip to eyebrow. he pulled a sheet of paper out of his suit pocket. looked at it. said it was the wrong speech, like later that evening he was going to an awards ceremony or specialist conference to present his findings. he opened his suit coat to search the inner pockets. piles of papers pressed against his ribcage. i imagine they are bills, collection notices of debts from the day spilling, a trail, following.

eventually he found the speech he'd written for this occasion. the whole fumbling papers bit, an old gag, he didn't even look at the paper, a vaudevillian set-up man in between acts; a sad clown before a buxom burlesque number.

my father welcomed everyone to the party. thanked the families and out-of-town guests for traveling the diaspora. he mentioned, as he does now when she comes back to Chicago to visit a couple times a year and they are in the same room for an awkward hour or two, how beautiful his ex-wife looks. nine years divorced then. it was really a beautiful speech. my father talked about his parents, George and Pearl, whose hearts collapsed in Chicago streets at different times somewhere before we were born, how today they would be proud to see their grandson follow in the tradition of his ancestors, how . . .

of course, at this time, my brother is lost in some distant coping mechanism, not paying attention to any of the speeches, conducting an ancient samadhi one-point meditation, staring at his feet, looking at the crowd, hoping for a gang of bandits to stick up the train wreck of his adolescence.

my grandfather speaks next. my mother's father who told my father, while my parents were dating, shit or get off the pot. (i guess he shit.) Papa was a wide and mean man. vengeance strapped to him like an army duffel. he leads off with a crack about how cheap my dad is. how his more financially sound sister had to help pay for the party. the kids at the party are comatose, but the cameraman finds these comments odd, so he pans the crowd, adult faces frozen in awe. my father's side amused, ashamed.

uncle Stephen is after Papa. he flew in from New York. he is my mother's brother. a writer, bike messenger, personal trainer to Roberta Flack and the New York school abstract expressionist painter Larry Rivers, whose daughter he'll eventually marry and divorce. Stephen left for New York years ago due to differences irreconcilable with his father's racist, xenophobic paternalism during Vietnam. but now Stephen is using his airtime at my brother's bar mitzvah to reconcile and recount and bring up all this old shit. he is speaking in generalities like aging and wisdom, and it is sadder knowing papa died not long after, too soon to undo the years of silence and brooding.

i am the next to give a speech. i am big-nosed and awkward. i am angry and sixteen. i have just read Malcolm and sworn off judaism. why i was allowed to attend, much less speak, remains a mystery. i start with a bit visible from a hundred clichés away. *i was told to come up here and say something nice about my brother* predictable pause the length of an asshole, *well . . . thank you, folks.* i walk away, the crowd unmoved, underwhelmed, a bit embarrassed at my dumbass-ness. my exit is a guise, of course, i turn around as if the hook that removes flops from the spotlight has returned me for more. i cry in the locker room when practice is over, after everyone has left. i have never told this to anyone. i am sixteen and have been let go from three jobs. i am running through a list of fabricated good times my brother and i have had. i invent on the spot. improvise, increasingly nervous. i end with a rant about a pagan ritual, a goat slaughtered, a skull of blood. there is disbelief and nothing funny.

my brother is unmoved. i grab his head and kiss his forehead, my big finish. he learns to iceberg, tread water, watch all the men in the family fall back on their schtick.

the speech i should've written
OR, the poem i said i would write for his 22nd bornday
OR, something for my brother at 32

today they say you are a man
then why did mom have to drive
you here?   seriously.

i regret selling our baseball cards.
i still owe you money for them.

i owe you a lot of things.

you were living in mom's basement then.
i was returning to sophomore year broke.

you have a family now.
you are moving.

remember when you locked yourself in the garage? no one could find
you for hours. mom had to leave her city job. your elementary school
called me at the junior high and asked if i knew where you were. you
were sleeping in white shorts and a white shirt on the garage floor cov-
ered in soot. when they told me you were safe i was so happy i partici-
pated in class that day.

it is true you did not drink drano.
you did get drunk in iowa though
and stumbled down main street, arms slung around
Bart Friedman's shoulders and mine, slurring
i love you guyssssss

you don't know this
but when i came into the house behind the gas station the night before
i left for college you were on the couch. the house dark, save the blue
flicker of tv. i had just gotten back from riding my bike around the
neighborhood with a hunting knife. i wanted to hurt something that
night, myself i think. something possessed was pedaling. i saw myself
from the perspective of a cinematographer. my body a stubborn actor.
when i returned and saw you and the worst i had done was scream in
the forest preserve at the moon, we wept. you remember. snot-out-the-
nose weeping. i was going to throw up.
but there we were   alive.

At the Passover Seder

the family is in full hilarity. fifty-plus cousins, uncles, and wide-hipped aunts packed into the basement of the Doubletree Inn in Skokie, Illinois. none of us actually live in Skokie anymore. we go back for nostalgic reasons. but i'm not sure we'll go back next year 'cuz at the end of the first night my cousin Rosalie, the evening's coordinator and mistress of ceremonies, gets into a fight with the manager of the banquet hall over a corkage fee. see Jackie and Marvin bring Manischewitz in huge jugs, jugs with twist-off caps, jugs that look like forties for Goliath, but because they are so big the manager wants to charge us four corkage fees per jug and Rosalie isn't playing that. she starts screaming and says the manager can stand on his head and whistle show tunes out his ass but she's not paying.

this is at the end of an already ridiculous evening. we sit in a U shape at our seders, partly because there are so many people and we all want to face the leader of the seder, but also because half the family doesn't talk to the other half. this one didn't get invited to that one's wedding, Lois forgot to call Netty on her birthday, Charlotte's son just got out of prison and hasn't come over for dinner (mind you he's fifty and lives in Arizona), sisters don't speak to sisters, but they're all in the same room at every occasion.

our cousin Floyd is getting married after years of a rather conspicuous life as a bachelor. he really does live in Skokie but also has an apartment downtown to entertain the ladies. when i was sixteen he handed me a hundred-dollar bill and said *party your balls off*. essentially he's a jewish kid who watched the *godfather* trilogy too many times and thinks it's acceptable to still wear Mr.-T gold and have your shirt unbuttoned to your nipples. you'd think everyone would be happy for him. he's found a nice girl to settle down with. G-d bless her—of course she's not jewish so everyone starts in on that and then Mike, who's not even related to us but goes to more family functions than i do, leans over to me between prayers and asks from what zoo did Floyd liberate her.

cousin Jackie works at the cosmetics counter at Carson Pierre Scott and looks exactly like the poet Gregory Corso and won't sit down all night. she's walking around pouring wine and water, clearing dishes, refilling maror bowls, waiting to open the door for Elijah, and the whole time, she keeps talking: *the tzimmes is good* she says *for bowel movements, works for me every time.* she's seventy-one and cusses like a drunk plumber. she's encouraging everyone to try her new lotion, *it's so good it makes your hands feel like a baby's ass.*

my Aunt Joyce is elbowing my dad in the ribs 'cuz he keeps eating the chocolate-covered toffee matzah before dinner and my brother is flashing me the finger and throwing gefilte fish at our cousin Geoffrey and we are all singing and praying and responsive to the call cousin Cheryl, who is leading the seder, makes for the participation necessary for this ritual meal.

in the haggadah, it says in each generation new freedoms are revealed. it says the younger generation will push the older generation, challenge injustice, demand we grow as a community to become more inclusive and humble.

there are many young ones at our seder table. we sit among four generations; cousins new to life, those at or past bar- and bat-mitzvah ages. no one is silenced. they are running around playing and talking and at some point in our service, the younger generation asks the elders four questions, asks that we explain the ritual, our purpose here, why we gather this night and do things the way we do. each new generation here to keep the elders honest.

ode to the gefilte fish

my grandfather would eat dozens
at a time out of jars like cookies.
gelatinous bone jelly dripping
from his fingers like honey.

around Pesach i look forward
to the story of our people devising liberation
strategies and this loaf of fish on a glass plate
a sliced, boiled carrot on top, perhaps, a mound
of horseradish, the mush of hot mess
sliding down my throat like mucus.

gefilte fish is the perfect food
for a wandering people, weaving around
europe with sacks, scrounging scraps
seaside, a boatload of cuttings, unwanted
bones and guts, a mish-mash of whitefish
carp, pike, anything with protein that's kosher
patty-caked with matza crumbs, discarded bits
the baker would throw away, put to use.

an environmentally forward Ashkenazic hamburger of sorts!
a culinary amalgamation! a Yiddish for the palate!
a chit'lins of the shtetl!

gefilte means stuffed!
i eat them like doughnut holes
until i live up to the name.
they are not sweet. they smell
like sweaty asses at the shvitz.
but in one ground nugget

a day's nutrients. a touchstone
in diaspora, a testament to perseverance
and the ingenuity to live
with stank breath.

my bubbe in the backyard
wears a gas mask, grinding horseradish
from scratch to lather these beige balls.

this salty bland doorstop of a main dish.
the messiah will come before it's reinvented
on celebrity cooking shows.

and i hate to say this
but it is the golem in the room
and my nose is already too big.
i can't afford to tell a lie . . .
gefilte fish looks like balsa wood
took a shit

    but tastes like history.

my grandfather is dead.
i eat to honor stories he never told me.

this flawed, lovely creation
tastes so much like home.
bitter. sweet.

hamotzi on thanksgiving

the goyim eat early.
at two their tables fill.
ham and creamed canned things.

we say between six and seven and actually
get to sitting around eight. there are meatballs
in a pot of brown liquid. spicy and sweet
a recipe some grandma stuffed in her purse
leaving austria.

our table is piled with plates.
the stuffing made with challah.
Jackie made it. she is eighty and still works
the perfume counter at Carson's.
she's gotta be there at four the next morning.

the whole table has come from elsewhere
on another first night we gather
without our Matriarch.

Gitta, her friend, is still here. she is
very much alive and sharp. on
the ride to her apartment
on Lake Shore Drive, she tells me
she escaped the hitler at seven.
she says it like this: *the hitler.*
here she is sitting next to me, talking
about her life as a producer:
Angels in America at the Royal George
the Jeff Committee, six kids
none of whom she is with.

we are all strangers.

the youngest at the table is Sasha
a blond, blue-eyed boy, boundless
in energy. he is six. earlier, in the front yard
while raking leaves and jumping over the pile
like an olympic event, he screamed
to the stars, *this is the very best*
thanksgiving ever in unpronounceable *r*s
that sang like *w*s.

his mom, the new matriarch
whose home we are in, a home
the bank foreclosed on
making this table of jews
squatters again, ready
to leave at any moment, again
adopted the boy Sasha from the Ukraine
twelve miles from where our Zadie George was born
a land from which he and his family fled the cossacks.

our table made from blood and forced movement.

Sasha will play *g-d*
bless america on the shofar.
before we eat, he reminds the table
of prayer, as the plates and people settle
at the table Bubbe Pearl used to feed the family
on the old West Side.

Sasha leads this table
of jews who have nowhere else to go
in prayer. the hamotzi on thanksgiving

the prayer for bread, the most frequently said
hebrew blessing. in a foreign land, in a foreign tradition
we are singing this ancient foreign holy language softly
this prayer thanking the universe
for bringing forth bread.

we are thankful for the integration
of our practice with the practice of our hosts
for the first time, we can sing hushed
in a home not our own. we thank G-d
for challah in the stuffing
we thank G-d for hybrid.

we say the hamotzi on thanksgiving.

this blessing
this curse

Rosh Hashanah in the Suburbs
OR, in the assimilated diaspora, it is still the new year!
OR, my brother cuts an apple, *Shana Tova!*

my brother is cutting an apple
in his house in mount prospect
on the second night of Rosh Hashanah

it is fall
harvest.
apples crisp
and small.
dipped in sweet
for the new year

it is 5772
though my brother calls it 2011

he says taffy apples are piled in the hundreds
at the entrance of Mariano's fresh market.
there, in the beginning of the new year
a man dances with sweet wands all day.
he is: an ascetic dipping, twisting apples on a stick
an immigrant body routinized, a labored mechanic
a fisherman with an eternal lure casting
calling our longing for ritual and sweet.

my brother is cutting an apple
on the second night of Rosh Hashanah
next to his blonde and christian wife
next to his blonde daughter
who is half of what i am

and more. who knows
what longing, desire, memory
we carry.
what need for iron
and fire
our cells demand.
a yearning to tell
to sit and listen
to delight, to raise the fruit
of harvest to one's lips with sweet

my brother is cutting an apple
tonight. he is jewish.
his son, upstairs sleeping, will not be
bar mitzvahed.

the knife is sharp
and decisive.
the apple splayed
in sections
passed around the table
raised to our lips, a prayer
maybe even slips, a little
mundane and G-dly. one
tiny tangent that tomorrow
will be, will be better, the children
will be healthy and sleep well.
an errant hope, maybe
a utopian dream
simmers. the desire
for sweet
honey and harvest.
head of the year

Rosh Hashanah.
in our crown, Keter
above consciousness
we sometimes move
unknowing or directed
or both. we move
are moved
by muse
music
magic.

my brother is cutting an apple
on the second night of Rosh Hashanah
and sharing the half-moons of sweet
with his family around the table

it is 5772
it is 2011

it is certainly
this moment

Shana Tova!
Shana Tova!

writing

for my father on Yom Kippur

if you work on the day the eternal book gets written will your name
    appear
if you eat too many pork chops, covet too many waitresses
if you default on too many promissory notes, rushing from bank to
    bank, seeking
    advances, loans, someone to understand
if you are struck down by stress this year, will this book and its author
    health care, will the government, will your lack of liquidity be an
    issue
    your slow cash flow, your floating of checks, your robbing of peter?

Pop, did you hear this year's ram's horn
on the day the book of eternity is written in grand temples?

    you are working.
    you are convincing newcomers in cubicles
        to give you house keys
        their dog to walk, the dog's shit
to pick up,   you old conniver
                genius entrepreneur
                you turn shit into green/C.R.E.A.M.
                Hashem makes fertilizer
                you make a living.

        all this is to live

    you song-and-dance
    for sorority girls and their cubs-fan husbands.
    Uncle Danny, they'll call you

                polite in their living rooms
                as you ask about where they come from
          you ask this of everybody but they don't
                talk to people outside of their condo association
                                you old swindler
                                making them laugh a little
                                as they agree to pay you $7
                                an hour

if the banks are open how can you rest
          in line trying to hustle a sympathetic junior account manager
          calling bill collectors, no one to listen to your payment program

your family can fast this holiest of mondays
on purple cushions in the conservative synagogue
wonder why you are absent and hope
your name appears in the eternal book

wonder your fate, Pop
on this day there is no dealing with money
but you are constantly dealing with money

and who will atone for that?

and i will atone for you
          if you can't

i will account for you
while you try to accrue an accountant

i am writing today, Pop
on the holiest of days
to ensure your name gets written

today

you are working
and i am a writer

working

in solidarity

on this day

writing
your name

assimilation &
its dis / contents

"It's weird, we ain't even supposed to be here."
Jay-Z

treif

the story goes like this:

in 1956
a convention of conservative rabbis
meets at the Palmer House in Chicago.
my cousin Jackie Hilliard, a cantor
turned *Borscht Capades* vaudevillian entertainer
has just sung some *nigums* to the thunder
of applause and tears

after he leaves the wooden podium
a Palmer House emblem glued to its front
hands are washed, prayers recited, a list
of *mozels* from the auxiliary board president
salad plates are cleared, the main course's silver top
removed to reveal sliced beef.

the ballroom packed with steak
knives screeching, forks scraping
ice clinking, the roaring chitchat
of rabbis and their wives.

Rose, Jackie's wife, a squat and somewhat fleshy
woman weighed down by gold and glee, stops chewing.
spits the baked potato into her napkin, subtle
as car backfire. her table is horrified. she stands
on her chair wrapped in rented linens and announces
her lungs blowing with the force of a shofar blast:

THERE IS BACON IN THE BAKED POTATO!

for a moment her sermon shakes the Palmer House
chandeliers like rain
                    then a flood
of rabbis and their wives pour from the ballroom
as if fleeing Pharaoh, crazed
to find the nearest bathroom
to stick fingers down their throats
and throw up
all that isn't kosher.

why jews celebrate christmas

i.   it's the only time of the year all my mom's people could get off work.
ii. it's a production.
    a.   my grandma's spread took days to lay out.
        i.   swedish meatballs in a hot and sweet brown sauce. brisket *au jus* (of course). mustard dip. farfalle primavera. caramels, cookies, and plenty of vodka.
iii. the main event was held just off the dining room.
iv. the adults gathered for highballs and martinis (even though my grandfather, a liquor salesman, never drank).
v.   this was the night he worked all year for.
vi. a room of family and a wall of presents that cost money he made.
vii. proof he provided for his children and grandchildren.
viii. things you could touch and say *my papa gave me this, this thing.*
ix. this was the night he felt most american.
x.   most fully
        free.

a christmas tale writes itself

the first year we moved into the big house in the suburbs near a pond, my parents got a christmas tree. three years later we would not live there or together. i was four, my brother seven months. i remember garlands and ornaments and leaving cookies for santa knowing my dad would eat them regardless. during decoration a pine needle went into his eye, almost blinding him. he wore a patch eating cookies and milk in the late hours of december twenty-fourth, alone. it was the last christmas tree we ever raised.

no juden

my grandfather didn't want any
jewish music at my parents' wedding.

he was a german jew. he hated
the nazis and he hated the jews.
an orphan, he hated the poor
homes he was raised in. he hated
the synagogues in Rogers Park.
he hated all the gentiles whispering
kike jokes, picking on his jewish friends
gassing him to the boiling point.

he said my dad's cousin, Jackie Hilliard, couldn't sing.
guests were not to hear the *hava nagila*. no horah
at the Drake Hotel, an order he barked. the horror, he thought
of such a scene: shtetl jews cavorting with vodka in circles.

my parents were doomed from the beginning:

my mother's father's family; first-wave german
jews who'd lived in america long enough to use the n-word
build a nest egg and whitewall their white fences.

my father's people; eastern europeans
running for their lives, entering this country
in the blues, in the emergent jazz age
which is to say improvisation, making it
up and over and fresh, a funky pidgin.

my father's folks were in Waldheim
before his wedding day, so my Aunt Joyce

my #1 aunt, my dad's only sister
a whole bat-mitzvah older, went to war
for not the last time, with my grandfather
my mother's father. she said to him
quoting a prominent midrashic interpretation
strewn thru much of Exodus (*and i'm translating*
here) my Aunt Joyce said to my grandfather
regarding the removal of jewish ritual
from my parents' wedding, my father
unable to stand up for himself, to such
a bully, such an unhappy, torn man

my aunt said to him, my grandfather
at the rehearsal dinner the night before my parents' wedding:

Go fuck yourself, Sy

> & the glass broke
> & Jackie sang
> & the guests circled
> & the guests danced
> as they did in the temple

Explaining Hanukkah

flippantly, perhaps in a foul mood, a sonorous old man appropriate
for the occasion. a grouch, she said, my girl from the south
of Illinois who didn't know any jews, which I thought impossible
in the age of Seinfeld. i rattled off something about the Joneses
the Applebee's. hanukkah being some minor holiday until jew
americans upped the ante cuz the ginormity of jesus's bornday
which fell near the end of the roman calendar culminating in work
stoppage and retail onslaught and the elders of cul-de-sacs
wanted jew american babies to feel right at home, though we are
trying to figure out where that may be.

eight days of gifts mystifies the christ kids
they think they've been left out this bonanza. this is not actually true.
the eight. i guess it depends on the family. in Wildbrooke, the fenced-in
hovel of Northshore McMansions, kids got cars at thirteen or some
shit. a series of impossible-to-get gadgets; a VCR in '82, a beeper in
'85, a cinder-block cell phone in '90. that was the desert of my
mother's struggles, she was sweet and ingenious, those days we
rounded our ranks to three; me, my brother and moms against the
world, its stable of state bureaucrats, landlords particular
about the first, my grandparents threatening to take us away.

the all-time highlight of my hanukkah gift-getting career was a
transformer: a robot hero or villain who moves through the world in
mundanity, living life as a car or laundry machine (i had the off-brand
bootleg version, not the trademark hollywood model), but through the
course of time, this can opener or cash register when called to rise to
action becomes a mechanical cockroach with lasers, changes to alter
the regime of the banal.

hanukkah meant latkes and menorah decorations from Osco hung in

the fourth-grade classroom of our public school with its new directive
of multiculturalism. at the ranch house turned rabbi lair of hebrew
memorization, songs and dreidel games. kids of working parents
couldn't afford the legit Temple Shalom located humiliatingly across
the street, huddled in the den-cum–rec room around the spinning
four-sided wooden top, waiting on *shin* to drop like shaking seven in a
game of craps. the winner retrieved gold-foiled chocolate gelt strewn
across the floor like Augustus Gloop the greedy fat kid in Willy Wonka's
factory. he was a fictitious german. we were real american   jews.

on one of the eight nights my dad's family would have a party for
some sixty-odd cousins packed into a huge home of the lone cousin
with hair, who was a real success. he hit in stocks or something lucky,
became a neoconservative who visited israel every year to plant trees
and hate Arabs, and would offer his castle for our challah baking.
inevitably some pair of old sisters would drink too much and fight
and stop talking to each other for the year to come. young cousins
would sneak to a bedroom to play truth or dare. the middle milieu
would stand in corners gossip whispering about who was cheating,
failing, birthing, buying, how much, what, and who for candlelight
well past kaput.

my mom's dad would roll all eight days into Christmas Eve, the night
america gave him off. a giant wall of wrapped boxes in the living room,
a brisket in the oven. on this night he was able to hand out i-love-yous
in silver and blue foil, green and red bows.

hanukkah is a story of war, i tell my girl.
in america, this is what we celebrate.

how jewish boys get irish names

I

his death certificate reads:
George Marcus Coval. my father
thought his father's middle initial
a V on crutches
stood for Murphy.

death certificates don't lie like jews
who grew up in irish neighborhoods.
a russian boy, squat and dark, had to hide
four clovers in the bush, circumcisions
in the public pool. Murphy not Marcus
so Micks with baseball bats won't hit like
Mantle. he even dropped the George
and walked to school with the O'Connell twins
red-freckled, horseradish in his lunchbox, red
like his Uncle Karl.

the boys and blonde girls would call him, new
and anointed, his American dream name: Murphy
like the bar behind the bleachers at Wrigley Field
where Hack Wilson and Gabby Hartnett and Tinkers
and Evers and Chance all played america's game
and all were not jewish.

2

jewish boys get irish names
so america will call us son,
                              too.

3

when I asked my mom
why she picked *Kevin*
she said it was her favorite
name.

not Seymour, her father
or Red, her father's best friend
not Moses or David or Saul
or Solomon or Ben or Avi
or Abraham or Ira or Adam

but irish and alliterative
with George's last name
chopped and anglicized
at the Island.

jewish boys get irish names
cuz our mothers have learned
not to want us
with women who look like them
who worry and cook and round
wide at the ass with hips. an irish
name might get us a Barbie, a spot
in a college with jew quotas, a raised
rung on the ladder out of the shtetl
and Skokie, an irish name blurs white
lines we won't have to wait in, we might
go right to the front of the bank, president
or at least top advisor, we might be able
to eat in any diner and neighborhood, we
might be welcomed for once, and stay, we

might not have to look over our shoulders, we
might be able to sleep thru the night and not rise
and run with pre-packed bags in the corner, in case, we
might be able to stay for a while and live and go to school
and cook and raise children and have a family
house that isn't burned down, books on the shelves
for generations, not ash, our generations not ash, we
might not be ash, or be bashed or bask in the glow
of burning temples and bodies and books and we
might pass and hide and pass and hope and hide
breathless in the attic and madeleine albright, all night
hoping not to disturb the quiet, which is not
irish but english, which is roman and colonial
which is ironic, that we might quiet
syllables rumbling in the backs of our throats
under heavy breath and tongues and hebrew
names, ironic we might not remember a language
we whispered in for five thousand years, we might want
whiteness and hide our names in the flat vowels
of the west cuz america is scared of what it can't
pronounce and we are Moshé and Binyamin,
Chaim and Abner, Efrayim and Eitan and Levi
and Malachi and Phineas and Shlomo and Yonatan
Yehudi, Yosef, and Chaya and Aya and Tikva
Nissa and Nitza, Leah and Miriam, Malka and Liat
Abrianna, Hosanna, Ilana, and Jezebel

4

O James Baldwin
the price of the ticket
is the Midwest accent
plain like the wheat fields

hill-less prairies, no Mount Sinai
or Zion for eternity!

Jimmy call me Melek
and I will call you king
hold you in my mouth
so everyone will know
your name, like mine, for once
cuz once america knows
your name they will be
comfortable with mine
and everyone who is
awkward in the mouth
on the tongue we taste like hummus
and mustard/greens and pickles
and we delight in our oddness
but america is too wonder bread
for our funk, our names fag and kike
treif on america's processed diction,
its tongue too bumpy too yellow to hold
us in their mouths, but we are in their mouths
Jimmy, you and I, whether they like it or swallow
us whole like putz and jive and slang
in their mouths like meshuggah and madness
and mad freshness and if it wasn't for us
would they ever laugh or dance or fuck or
say anything other than other *other* and we
ourselves are so different, but Jimmy
you were my father when I was bar-mitzvahed
in the bath house, in mixing-pool diasporas, jumbled
along the way to find my name, Melek like Africa
like twisted and syllabic, a carnie at the fair
telling america how much her name will cost
in your mouth when you sing

allegory of the jewish boy served pork at his friend's restaurant

cuz Roger Bonair-Agard

at some point you want to be cared for.
all night the bartender, a blonde (of course!)
who makes her own bitters and sour mix
from scratch, is muddling sweet
and herbs to make bourbon some summer
time elixir, some alchemy, some magic.
the people you came with are chest up
to the bar and chatty. they are all christian
and/or some brand of american diet.

at this point, it's not an issue.
the salad is roasted asparagus
beneath a runny egg and crostini.
there are sides of spicy fried chickpeas
some duck confit you can avoid.
the issue arises when you are four
drinks in and the bartender has been
maybe helping herself some too
so she when asks *what you wanna do
next*, you say *surprise me* or something
trite and she takes you up on that.

she slides before you a martini
glass that reeks of barnyard.
you aren't sure what it is.
she can tell, she's good at reading
people. she says it's whiskey infused
with bacon smoke and vanilla.
she explains how this happens.
you are not listening.

there is a problem. you are
wondering how one captures ghosts
(you are definitely not bill murray
more harold ramis and no one here
even knows who he is!) and the bartender
is done explaining. she asks what you think
and thank G-d there are a few
droplets left of the last cocktail.

the conversation resumes
tho you have left it. you wish you could
knock the glass over or break it
mazel tov! you wish you could run.
you are silent and the smoke is wafting.
you are always strange in this land
of milk and meat. last time there were bits
of bacon in your baked potato, you threw up
in the bathroom and never told anyone.
you want to break the glass, but are contemplating
the commandments. you do not want to cause
a disturbance, a moment of dis-ease, how many times
does america force you to choose, treif and profane.
the whole country is a Michigan bar
forty minutes outside Detroit, miles from home
-less, down home. dark wood. a foodie haven
written about in travel magazines. the chef
has a quartered pig tattooed on his forearm.

there is not a break
in the conversation.

you are sweating now.
your friends are laughing and gay.
they don't know

you refuse shellfish even tho yr girl thinks it's ridiculous.
they don't know
    you hate x-mas. sincerely
    feel retribution certain each easter. all history
    points to this. the passion play's long procession
    outside every day. every year:

say Leo Frank
say Joe McCarthy
say Menahem Mendel Beilis
say some camp you heard a thousand times.

you know the final solution was still in your grandfather's lifetime
and most of the people who sit at the bar didn't say shit
but left you stuffed into boxcars
like pigs.

where do jewish boys go when they shave their beards
        and marry shiksas?
where do jewish boys go when country clubs bubble
        with christians?
where do jewish boys go when the temples are burned
        by all of joe lieberman's friends?

tonight is the sabbath.
the drink is in your hand.

say bottoms up
say l'chaim
say life upside down
say this country
    every diaspora
    not zion.
say israel

not zion.
say some segregated
    kibbutz. a dream.
    some fake other-
    world.
say israel
    a christian country
    club.

the jewish boy wants
a place to be jewish.

say nebbish
say minutiae
say long particular orders at restaurants
say shabbos
say kaddish
say kiddush
say kadosh
say 22 letters
say 18 is life
say l'chaim

    a place to be jewish.

say cheers
where everybody knows
your hebrew name.

an american parody:
in parts

un/doing the pyramids

> *A large, massive, club-shaped, hooked nose,*
> *three or four times larger than suits the face. . . .*
> *Thus it is that the Jewish face never can [be],*
> *and never is, perfectly beautiful.*
> **Robert Knox, anthropologist, 1850**

Jakob spent nights sleepless staring at the bridge
of his sister's nose. meditating in the emergence
of a growing nationalist party. a mad doctor
digging morgues to practice on cadavers.
the surgery is complicated. the correction
requires *lowering of the dorsum, narrowing*
the bony pyramid, refinement and elevation
of the excessively long hanging tip.[x]

Jakob Joseph made wounds less horrendous. a magician
of skin, awarded an iron cross for using the pristine
smooth of foreheads to patch the scars of amputees.

Jakob, son of Rabbi Israel and Sarah
born in Germany. a surgeon who amended
deformities of the first war as rumblings
of the second grew.

Jakob called the desire to look normal
anti-dysplasia. against the displeasure
of the rabbi for mutating the body G-d
gave. correcting the jewish nose
which displeased the german gentry

---

[x] F. V. Nicolle, *Aesthetic Rhinoplasty* (London: W. B. Saunders, 1996).

the offense of the large olfactory.
Jakob saw jewish peasant girls
and altered their faces for free.
they could seek employment
outside the shtetl, change
their name, abridge their history.
marry a german general.   live.

Jakob figured how to remove
the knot on the bridge, undo the pyramids
slaves built. narrow *the acute nasolabial angles* . . .
foreshorten [the] nasal[N] passage to pass
into the plateau and platitudes
of aryan social balls.

Jakob disguised the nose and face-
d the facts: moving ahead
you hide.

[N] E. Matory, *Ethnic Considerations in Facial Aesthetic Surgery* (Philadelphia: Lippincott-Raven, 1998).

making it, more or less

for my #1 aunt

I

Joyce never would've got hers done
if it weren't for Manny Pine, manager
of the Barry Sisters, beautiful brunettes
like Joyce, who cut Yiddish records. formerly
the Bagelmans, born in the Bronx, the sisters
toured the country in sequences holding slender
microphones beneath their more slender noses.

they were at the Royal Theater on 45th Street
where *Borscht Capades* sold the house
weeks at a time. Joyce was the road manager.
rare for a young woman to move around so much.
a thirty-five week run in Miami before New York.
she was unencumbered by mid-fifties gentile sensibilities.
this is showbiz! *after the Shoah, who cares anyway*
                              Manny said.
backstage as the night really began to buzz
standing beneath pulleys holding sandbags.
union men shlepping, actors, singers, ventriloquists
whirling thru the revolving stage door in this Yiddische
variety show. house lights raised and falling
flicker like candles on the faces in the wings.
Manny leans in close enough for spittle to sprinkle
Joyce's cheek, whispering he'll take her down
town where the sisters had theirs done
                              Manny says
a beautiful girl like you shouldn't have a nose like that.

2

Joyce eventually went home
to her immigrant mother
whose nose was a wondrous
waterfall of a beak, the tip
almost able to feed her mouth.

Joyce asked her mother
if she could cut her nose.

her mother, Pearl, understood
how this country worked.
she worked in it. knew
someone who knew someone
at the hospital where she worked
one job. where two
doctors in Chicago
did this kind of thing.
Brown and Becker, both
on Lake Shore, the beautiful
drive where mansions
were built, the people here
made it. Pearl would
make sure Joyce could
make it here. one day
she brought her only daughter
to one of these surgeons
who could make her more
by making her less, by making her

more or less   american.

punch line

mike kagan would call her Zorro
the way her nose could cut a Z thru the air.

at thirteen and fourteen she wore size 13 and 14.
her brothers, olympians.
her mother, runner-up Mrs. Illinois.
her father wanted a boy.

every spring break
skokie took to transforming
the faces of little girls.
bandages, bruises, swollen
magic

at fifteen and a half she asked
her parents for a new nose.
it must've been after dinner
her brothers dismissed
to romp in the front yard
under streetlights.
her parents said *finally*.
made an appointment
with Dr. Lazar.

fifty years later
she still wants work done.
fillers to tighten her face.
liposuction on the arms.
there are entire nights
with her second husband she is uncomfortable.
she thinks there are prettier people in the room

and the man she came with might as well.
born to the GI and housewife
jews who made exodus
just north of Howard.
fit and pomade
constant quaff
and airs. a lincoln
in the driveway
the workingman's
cadillac.

postwar posters
pushing their newborn
baby girl in a stroller
down bob-o-link.
the neighbor lady tootled
from her second-floor flowerbed.
raced downstairs
to greet this beautiful couple
fresh back from the hospital.

a fall afternoon.
my grandpa in tweed and sweater vest.
my grandma in a skirt with flats and a cardigan.
the neighbor lady bent in the basket
where my mother lay, newly alive
exclaimed
what a beautiful . . .
    afghan

aghast
    polite. quiet.

my mother knows this story
cuz her mother tells it to her.

it could've been
left out of her history
book.   instead
she has been trying to erase
herself
for/ever
after.

remembering baby: an american parody (in parts)

I

at the eighty-first annual Academy Awards
Jennifer Grey is a guest of her father
Joel, Tony Award–winning originator
of the master of ceremonies role in *Cabaret*.

on this night in February, Grey wears a black tux
on his thin frame, a white Sammy Davis
an entertainer. he could sing, tap, shuck
jive and schtick like his old man. a legit talent
a Yankee dandy cracking up Dean Martin
and the boys.

Jennifer is in black satin couture. eyes cut
Egyptian Liz Taylor, Michelle Pfeiffer's Cat-
woman. face sanguine and distant. she is
no baby in the corner, no older sister
making out with Charlie Sheen.
she hasn't worked since her work.
she is on the red carpet hoping to be seen.

2

i met her once, downtown
in the second restaurant that led to my father's

first bankruptcy. pre-op. post-up
in the heights over Patrick Swayze's head.

a jewish boy's jewish crush and dread.

she always went for Johnny's leather jacket.

i was a busboy clearing her table. she ate
one-quarter of a club sandwich, asked

for mint tea. i carried the steeping pot
to her hands splayed on the white table.

my father introduced us. she smiled
thanked me. her palm lithe in mine.

3

time has stretched since the Cleveland Playhouse
where Mickey Katz fathered the American parody
song. toured the Borscht Belt with a violin and plastic-
wrapped corned beef sandwich. Weird Al Yankovic's
orthodox master. Mickey revamped popular radio tunes
in Yiddish. first-seat jester in Spike Jones's orchestra.
Davey Crockett became Duvid. an album of greatest schticks.

Mickey begat Joel
who changed his name to Grey
made it further in the business.
didn't lead with his jewish.
an Oscar, a Golden Globe.
a fixture on Broadway.
Joel begat Jennifer.

4

her nose was long and curved
downward at the tip.

Eastern Europe
like my brother's, Poland.
operation one, botched. something horrible.
a smattered mess of jelly, flesh. butterflied filet.
a forced return to the table under lights, under knife.
the second made her unrecognizable
to fans and casting agents. Hollywood
hard luck. a lifetime of Lifetime. a rising
starlet of the big screen, remade for tv.
the aquiline nose she was known
for sculpted, small, bulbous. stone.
the beak obliterated. gone.

5

Oh Jennifer Grey!
where have you been all these years?
where did you hide, what kept you in?
tonight, before the mirror, before the parade
of cameras and litany of second looks and moments
of onlookers thinking they might remember you
from that thing you did somewhere, were you
tempted to tell the makeup artist
bring back the hump! retract the blade!
are there phantom itches on the bridgeless slope
of your nose? cross-eyed reveries? profile flashbacks?
do you ever put on Groucho's glasses and remember
you were so beautifully us?

Warhol Nose America

after Andy Warhol's Before and After I, *c. 1961*

the immigrant is GIANT.
a presence, undeniable
forehead (un)even, a rolling (century)
country/side. the beak:
a knife
a sickle
a chisel
the iceberg
that sunk the titanic.
a shaft small children
could fall in.
before . . . MIS-
SHAPED
MISS HAP'D
her name
corrected, reset
a small surgeon
ran the National
Enquirer. took
the *enlarged and projected*[N]
trimmed it
to proper size
and ideology.
RESHAPED
in the suburbs
to settle and quiet
amongst the o(O)ther
petites, almost
to the point
of blending.

[N] Text traced from the description at the Metropolitan Museum of Art.

No Nose Job
OR, How Humpty Put Me Back Together Again

dodio-doe, there'll be no nose job
said dodio-doe, no nose job
(i'm smarter than that)
—Digital Underground

live at the Apollo

in green pants and an orange flower blazer
gold dripping and whirling around him like a giant
swing at the carnival, Humpty has west coast funk
for an Apollo audience. home of CJ Walker
Humpty is selling something
Harlem is in need of. it is '92
Shock G is on some PE, on some millions
to hold back this nation, this history

the video: dream sequence

in a city hospital, Humpty
tries to escape. male nurses
foil his plan.   (DJ Fuze bumblebees' scratch)
the doctors are trying
to remove the hump
shorten his name
his nose

see, for me, the bigger the nose the better

the darker, the sweeter, the stanky-er
the funky-er, the less lite, the less white
the more original, more crooked and less
straight, the fresher, the flamboyant, the protruding
the rude-er, the rude-boy, the ravishing
the nose in everybody's bizness, the hook
and jab, the jew nose and smush-faced
and mush-mouthed and slang schtick
something Other than the same shit

ode to the schnozz

after Aracelis Girmay

oh gonzo! what length
what mucusy noise
to even muscle. what land of oz
what person behind the polar
cap. what plastic surgeon
eluded. what wondrous
slope, what ellis island kike cliff.
oh dago Jimmy Durante!
what majestic mound of cartilage
what crooked center of face. the bump. the kink
of neck it takes to kiss you. the tilt and beautiful
maneuvering. you know what they say about the size
of a man's giant   bridge for glasses. the grander
than roman. the grandeur. the semitic spatial abrasion
so big, cheeks double as bodybuilders.
the tip too often graced by tongue.
there is a toucan impersonation
in your future, a halloween
trick and groucho marx mask.
what wondrous past
this olfactory anomaly must
manufacture. what gas
what pickled brine
what stench
once cut thru
what raw fish
what raw flesh
what offense
so opulent to make such
a monument

Babs in Babylon

Is a nose with deviations
a crime against the nation?
Kay Medford as Rose Brice, *Funny Girl*

at the Lion in Greenwich the boys loved you.
all the boys, the fabulous ones who applauded
wild when you hit on Jack Paar in a long dress
with long notes and long nose. cleopatra eyes
fabulous
Babs
belting
in babylon. when you hit
the last note
and it was a good note
your mouth
opened and twisted
comedic. you knew, you killed it.
a jewish girl working
in front of the camera. all that
schnozz, all that jazz. a star
not starlet. long eyes
painted like comets, an orbit
in a different galaxy. the director of photography, a genius
to let light linger
long, sweeping side profiles. pause there
delight in the bump
beneath lights, the length and girth.
the thousands of faces you saved
from the knife, long nails
on the backside of america's libido.
seductress
pulling the long

low notes, high
belting a new
tune, you fame Us
fabulously

shiksas

shiksas

my father, home for the summer between college
tanned and balding already from lifeguarding
at the Carl Sandburg Apartments in old town.
his body rigid from the physical education majors'
required lifting with the football team, a student trainer
too tiny to middle lineback. he'd wrap ankles.

one night, the summer's heat and Chicago's humidity
demand fans and ice boxes open longer to linger
in front of. the night a warm bath of urine and lilac.
my father in the basement with Jenny Bundy a gentile girl, all blonde
over her naked. in high school he never had the confidence to ask her
out small and weak, a second-string second-base Senn Bulldog: but as
a college freshman, a miracle. a foot growth spurt, shoulders broad
stomach flat, Jenny Bundy noticed at Wells Park in the Connie Mack
summer league, floating around the diamond long after the game to let
my dad ask her to a movie, lead her to his parents' basement at 5629
North Kenmore in Edgewater, where Lake Michigan breezes die in the
cellar window, where Sabbath nights a minyan of cousins ate brisket
and played cards Tuesdays. a basement with a drain, linoleum, a dusty
orange couch Jenny Bundy swam nude on, my father's hands cool over
her hot skin, windows starting to steam

    and then the door cracks

and the light's on
and Pearl
loud and squat
hands of a meat packer, creaks on the top
two wooden stairs of the basement
Ethel Merman yelling

Danny is that the shiksa who gave you the clap?

my father puzzled, embarrassed, told to lose Jenny Bundy's number
went to his old man wanting to know why mom was mad, replaying
the sage wisdom he'd received returning from school, *pop I thought you*
told me to go out with a shiksa

my Zadie, George Marcus Coval
considered his son's confusion.
hands spread and pressed together before his face
two pointer fingers on his lips, the lightbulb flashed
picturing where his son went wrong.

George leaned forward in his chair
pushing up on raw, rubbed armrests. his arms now
spread wide over an invisible accordion, hands open
and shaking and up to heaven to catch rain or plead with G-d
why he has been forsaken with a son who is such a mo-mo
George, to his only hope of a continuing Coval name
says slowly in his immigrant Russian accent turned flat Chicago jew,
said arms now fully extended to the sky of apartment ceiling, *sonnyboy*
I said SHIKSAS

the merchant, the shiksa, and the american dream: the tropes of *Debbie Does Dallas*

mr. greenfield owns a sports store
though he wanted to be star quarterback
for america's team. blue stars
on silver helmets parading the texas prairie.
roger staubach and cheerleaders in short shorts
white vests, legs in unison kicking
the sky. mr. greenfield crunched
numbers, took inventory, watched
the game from the office
on tv. sold replica jerseys
and exercise equipment.

he was not fit enough.
a merchant, dreaming.

debbie dreamed the life
of a cheerleader in dallas:
dates with players. half-time
dances. blond, petite, long; debbie
barbie with a texas drawl, needed
money. mr. greenfield had it
for debbie. hired her to work
the store. paid to watch her
move thru aisles of national
pastime accoutrement; gloves
white balls, wooden bats.

at the end of the most popular pornography in all of adult cinema

mr. greenfield in pads and cowboy uniform
chases debbie, in full guise, midriff and miniskirt

around the store. pays her per act. circumcised prick
thru the hole of his tight pants. debbie
on the bench press, hat and tassels, frazzled
and fucked, the cheerleader calls his name
mr. greenfield, mr. greenfield
pumping till touchdown.

boxer

when she moved to hollywood
rebecca israel became becky boxer
and got prettier than she was in junior high
and blonder. a personal trainer. celery
sticks and slim-fast or something. smoker's
lips or something. sunken cheeks.
she tried to shiksa.

becky's dad, steve, a multimillionaire
retired in his thirties and coached little league.
maybe becky thought she had to be a boy
a boxer, an athlete, for attention.
            she slugged it out
on the west coast, alone
in studio, on call, casting
prayers, compulsively
checking phone messages
counting crackers. no mayo
in her tuna fish, yogurt
commercials, voiceovers
she'd do anything. her big
break is *jarhead*
with jake gyllenhaal.
a film about war
during war.
            larry hirsh told me
she was in the film.
he used to live near me
on the other side of a fence
in a big red home, in the suburbs.
now he lives in a loft in wicker park.

we had lunch at the milk & honey
cafe across the street. he said
his dad called him and told him
he now knows what he used to
look at. larry dated becky
or something and now is a real
estate something with money.
he said becky was in this movie;
something she'd been fighting
her whole life for. she is the girl
on tape, someone's wife taking it
hard on a camcorder, before a room
of jarheads. other than the moans
she has one line, but all you see is
becky getting fucked.

assimilation nightmare #1

                    paris hilton sits alone
neckline plunging like the san andreas fault.
her bottom lip bends ripe in the light, roma tomato
lip gloss luring my attention from the hotel barstool.

                    bourbon boosts my confidence.
i ask to sit beside her in the love seat
her glance dusts the open space.
her feet curl like spring. in a rush
my coattails brush her gown, white
and sheer. her nipples orange gumdrops
in the glass jar on my grandma's coffee table.

                    i pull a flower from my lapel
spray her with water, gnaw the wet end
of a cigar. tell quips; the one about
grant's tomb, what color the white house was.
her flash-ready smile dances along my arm
like flames. my nose keeps getting in the way
every time she leans in to kiss me.
but she doesn't seem to mind the thickness
of my eyebrows nor the rumors
of my communist sympathies.

                    the skyline is on fire.
we watch from the twentieth-story sitting room,
feet up on honey-striped ottomans, liquor
lacquered coffee tables, gold-nameplated
Latinos ask if we wanted a drink
or something to eat. everything but paris and me
is brown, surrounded in a swash of earth tones.

we giggle in the glow of red
sirens. the city reflects in the blank screens of her
eyes, staring out panoramic windows, watching
Los Angeles burn.

assimilation nightmare #2

Angelina Jolie is controlling my mind.
every time she opens the doors to her
limousine, the interior, fabric colored
like lollipop spindles, whirls to hypnotize.
my body, a magnet, dictates. my mind
makes out the menacing, but i am helpless
a walking Boris Karloff, unable to shy away.

she shows up at odd times. in the bread aisle
at Trader Joe's, wheat loafs tumble like bricks.
boarding the Blue Line, her sleek black low-rider
screeches before the station, i return to her lure
unable to slide through the turnstile. she is too
enchanting, her command cogent. i am forced
to leave birthday parties, staff meetings, dentist
chair cleanings, riled by her wiles, i am a night
of zombies, an extra in F. W. Murnau films
a mummy in Dockers goose-stepping toward her.

only Morgan Freeman can save me.

as Angelina pulls in front of the laundromat, something
tells me this'll be the last time i glimpse the outside world.
the white plastic basket belly flops to the ground, the doors
swing open like saloon gates; i inch toward them, a reluctant
prisoner dragging chains to the jailhouse. Wagner's
Das Liebesverbot pipes into the street.
                                            but
as my fingers are about to weave into hers for eternity
Morgan Freeman, roused from the corner, unzips his grey
workman jumpsuit, drops the mop and bucket (a disguise

the Secret Service devised for his co-star) and full sprints
jumps, cross-body blocks the hairline fracture between
Angelina and me, wrestled to the ground, spell broken
this daring man's life   risked   for my own.

inheritance

the find

seven days after the funeral
my father cleaned George's closet;
shirts, cufflinks, plenty of swim trunks
donated to the mt. sinai resale shop
and a leatherbound black album.

in the doorframe of the his dead father's bedroom closet my father flipped.

breasts spill page to page
like a slinky. a museum of flesh.
a cartographic study of suntan lines.
some look dead into the camera. some aloof
under studio light. some flash the photographer
on break rocks at the beach. all are beautiful
women of fifties and sixties Chicago, the home
of playboy. these clippings are originals
snapped by the man himself. in some George is
shirtless in black trunks. a wrestler
barrel chested and broad. hair
and body glisten in oil and sweat.
he stands with women
not his wife. sometimes two
at a time. their arms, a belt
at his torso, dance
like snakes in eden.

somewhere on the north side

in a small rental, on a wood floor
in the doorframe of his dead father's closet
my father sits cross-legged for hours.
buddha
beneath the bodhi tree.
lost
in each picture
entranced
in epiphany.

George

George ran lakeview printing
press. a monotony of metal letters
arranged by hand to make stationary
and local papers neighborhood men
would tuck under an arm in transit.

when Chicago was warm enough
George saw the city from a lifeguard chair
at Oak Street Beach. there is a family legend
he swam home to edgewater after his shift.
he loved the heat. a russian sun
g-d so dark he could pass as sicilian.

George developed a hobby.
snapped photos weekends
in south haven, passover seders
a couple of bar mitzvahs.

George the shutterbug
built a small studio at the printing press.
a makeshift one in a cabana at Oak Street Beach
it seems.

George lost Pearl to a heart attack.
George was calm. Pearl on fire.

George died living with a woman
who refused to call the ambulance
after a night of short breath
and chest pains. a woman
not my grandmother Pearl.

George speaks

well what can i tell ya, i like shiksas, sonnyboy, what's not to like?
Pearl, G-d rest her soul, was a pear, a bear of a woman. when we met
she was beautiful, sure. the most beautiful girl at the high school dance.
there were only jewish girls at the dance. jewish girls were the only
girls i'd ever meet. and who wants to be with a girl like your mother? not
me, oedipus rex, thank you very much. on the western bus, i'd see all
sort of girls. blondes, black girls, spanish puerto ricans. all these girls
were beauties. well not all em. but a lot of em. none of the jewish guys
ever really talked to em. they didn't know how. they were scared little
pisspants. wah wah. what did ya have to lose? and i got good at it. talk-
ing, i mean. i was a good lookin' guy. did calisthenics every day. swam.
i swam a lot. and i love vegetables, particularly peas. haven't had meat
since the forties. but i just got good at talking. there's not a lot to it. you
say hello. introduce yourself. ask where they are from. and there you are
on the western bus talking to a beautiful girl from somewheres else.

to ask a woman to pose for you naked takes some chutzpah.
you don't lead with the proposition. you glide into it. it's a dance.
with these women, there is silence. at home nothing but noise.
Pearl ran a community center. between her family
staying with us, all the cousins, the neighbors she'd take in.
i'd eat dinner with her yelling in my ear, *do this George do that George,*
are you going to take Nettie to the store
George, are you going to eat the brisket i made, are you
going bring home more money George. YELLING.
i'd pretend not to listen. i'd wait till she took a breath
and raise my finger and simply say *Danny will you pass the pepper?*
there was always noise in the house. arguments and pots whistling
jewish women talking and talking about their husbands and sons
and the insufficient cut the butcher gave them. i am a decent man!

94

quiet is a man's right. silence is the golden hair
of the shiksas i snapped. with all these women there was quiet.
quiet and skin. women who worked on their tans and kept their bodies.
these were american women, sonnyboy. and we live in america.

passdown

as Chicago beaches ready to open
on memorial day, i get the call. my father says
he wants to show me something.

the album sits on the kitchen counter like a tomb
when i enter my father's house.

we stand in the faint cool of humming
window units, turn each page in careful amazement.
the women are stunning. sweet and nude.
the photos a kind of innocence
compared to the raunch behind the cash
register at 7-11 or the *girls gone wild* DVDs
tucked into my father's underwear drawer. there is a sort
of kindness in the eyes that once looked in
to the camera where my grandfather once stood.

i stand there now
with my father
near an oven
beneath a ceiling
fan, fifty blocks from the pictures'
origin, fifty years ago.

we are silent
re-creating George's gaze
standing where he once stood.

midrash

all the women look nothing like my grandmother.
Pearl was short and zaftig. hips. bottom like a light
bulb. the photos must've been snapped while she was
alive, while they were living, together and married.
when my dad was a boy and George clandestine.
the women were buxom and alive and blonde. skin
like a dairy farm. they couldn't have been more
than forty or thirty or immigrant. in these photos
they are frozen and perfect. gorgeous and goyische.
all shiksas in the sunlight studio glow
of Oak Street Beach or Lakeview Printing.

i will never know what his voice sounded like
coaxing them into the cabana or how well
he knew their names. he was a dog, a mack, a g-d
of conniving, a hustler with a big shiksa
fetish that he'd photograph into still life
put on a pedestal, make timeless and leave
for his sons.

schtick

Don Rickles Roasts Ronald Reagan

he still
doesn't get
it.
    the jokes
are
over
      his head.

the jester
throwing knives
at this guy
    code
     vowel shift
this goy
     this one's
     for the kipper
some jew fish
double speak
in front of gentiles.

the governor is dumb
he says. period.
then jazz hands
and shimmy.
   is he laughing
the bald mean jew
makes him laugh
hair unmoved
something like card
board, propped
and whitened, all

the darkness lurks
backstage.

        it is 1985
now the second inaugural
ball, the cold war is on.
the jew is in the center.
the highlight of his career.

to billy graham:
nice to see you sir, this hand is bothering me . . .
i could've been a pitcher, if i talked to this guy

to charlton heston:
if you were Moses, I was a Mau-Mau fighter pilot!

to the secretary of state:
go over to the embassy.
have a bucket of beluga.

is this too fast, ronnie?[N]

all the hints
at something
wrong. the seat
near these goys
the hottest.
the grand dragons
burning beneath
the surface.

[N] All italics are Rickles's lines from Reagan's Second Inaugural Ball, January 20, 1985, at the National Air and Space Museum.

the jester knows
when to punch
and pull back
a fighter
pilot indeed
a master
of the masters.
a dump in their
house. some corn
ball and grease
slide these barbs
quick   jabs.
this whole
thing   a joke.

loaded

1

Sid Caesar was a giant
star—his most famous bit an imitation
of a german WWII general.
composed of gobbledygook
and Yiddish. on his hourlong show
live into the camera he spoke to the country
in nonsensical tongues of the eastern bloc.

early mimic.
son of immigrants.

he learned the music
of europe's languages
busing tables at his parents'
twenty-four-hour diner in Yonkers.

2

the lone character he couldn't
play was Sid Caesar. he'd twitch
a nervous fit of coughs
thru his show's intro
Good Evening Ladies and Gentlemen
I'm . . . (cough) . . . Sid (cough) . . . Caesar . . .

3

he assembled the most talented
consortium of comedic writers in american
history—Mel Brooks and Woody Allen

Neil Simon and Carl Reiner—around
a conference table of coffee and knish
jew heroes who poked at their predicament
their anxiety real.

he came to meetings loaded
with a revolver. convinced
the german general otto skorzeny
would surface in a submarine
on the east river and assassinate him
somewhere along 57th Street
or near a Hebrew National
cart or walking in the morning
dew of central park.

4

I'm a Polish janitor
I'm Isaac Sidney
I'm a post-Shoah clown
I'm an American jew
I'm Sid Caesar
I'm Odysseus in rags

5

otto skorzeny was a master
of disguise himself.
Sid Caesar's ss nemesis.
he liberated mussolini
dressed as a gondolier.
he led operation grief
and put german soldiers
in american uniforms

in american jeeps and drove
into allied forces
at the battle of the bulge.

after the war
skorzeny donned pseudonyms;
robert steinbacher, otto steinbauer.
built a safe passage for ss officials
to Argentina. wore mustache at a cafe
in the Champs-Élysées.

otto skorzeny was Sid Caesar
's mirror. the clown costume, inverted
stalking the periphery.

6

what else to do but laugh
around midtown
waiting to shoot german tourists
waiting for bombs to drop
waiting for offices to be raided,
homes bugged and ransacked
lives publicly scoured—Sid
was the janitor who sacrificed
Isaac at lunch hour with bourbon
and pills, anxious with waiting
for otto—an absurdist dream
become sub-conscious become
surface along the east river
as Sid walked down 57th Street—
revolver   loaded.

allen ginsberg gets expelled from columbia university for writing *fuck the jews* in dust on the windowsill of his dormitory

moloch! this great zion
prophetic koan, was it?
the beginning of the State
the writing on the wall

was it?
the closet
full of dead
roses, his mother
in the asylum
hearing Voices
was it?
the basement
full of socialists

the cock is certain
the balls endless
in the bathroom

i wd be a buddhist too

anything

but a jew

fuck them in dust
a temporary aside
a permanent rendition
a premeditation

fuck the jews

for moving to the suburbs
the settlements, for monsters
and moloch! and mainstream′
movies w/out yiddish subtitles

fuck the jews

for war bonds and banking
systems and congressional hearings
and closets and outrageous cocks
to suck and bedfellow allegiances
forged in Abel's blood

what dormboy doesn't
say this

what soldier doesn't
piss *this* into the sand

Dirty Names for Monica Lewinsky

zaftig
queen
    Esther—
such conspiracies say
netanyahu and falwell be-
came cohorts to jerk
clinton and the world's
attention twenty-four hours before
israeli-Palestinian negotiations.

while (white) houses were demolished
and settlements expanded, Monica went down
on an american president to save an israeli
prime minister.
    the whole thing   sounds dirty.
what brains
and forethought
what cojones and cabal
runs this joint
    (a big) but it happened—
the family connects, back
handshakes and perfect timing.

what fetish
to keep
the dress
the seed
spilled—
Genesis
38:8–10

Monica taught the president

to be a mensch, to eat nookie
good. this fat cracker
from arkansas who opened her
mouth and borders to nafta
and neocolonialism.

Monica the spy, the plant
the whore, the home wrecked
the fat kike, i'd love to watch
fucked by a goat[x]

Monica
dark and doughy
warm and rosy
kugeled and full-
lipped. wide-bottomed
and big-mouthed.
the anti-WASP
hillary rodham.
the intern with chutzpah
and warm tongue.
the adulterist who had done this
before—fucked a married dude—
the president of the country
club. Monica, the demon-
ized, the set-up, the linda tripp.
the messy age we impeach in.
Monica, the cherry popper
the olive sheep who will lie
like a man. she held
the world in the palm
of her hand.

---

[x] YouTube comment by #ThorOdinson14.

Mean Woman

an ode to Joan Rivers

you are the funniest person
on tv. i was gonna say woman
but i mean person.   you mean
a lot of things. that must happen
a lot. the misnaming. the plastic
alternations and alien appellations
for woman, for sure, for jew, maybe.

but you Trump all jabs with knockouts
the quickest combinations in the diamond
ring, silver screen. redefine what a craftsman is
i mean woman. you mean woman.

jokes scribbled and ordered
in dewey decimal card catalogues in the kitchen
a library, a hideout, an institution at this point
you always fresh, up-to-date, and in the future.
rehabbed on hallowed grounds, well traversed
the terrain of insecurity and grand loss.
a country and culture telling you *no*
your place woman, which you said is everywhere
asshole!

the roots bleached, but not rootless
ruthless. fat sucked, but you never do
perhaps hunched now on a couch
with whatever young host, you outshine
out-bling and bleep them. no one' can hang
cuz no one is that good

that free
to say what is

you keep telling us
you will die one day
that we will one day, too
but the material is timeless
timed perfect, always on time.
we take comfort in that, raised
in the lash cut of your tongue
the quick-wit song of the demented
the retarded. imperfection's revenge
and hilarious rage. the odd and left.
the abnormal song in jest
in slights, the sin, the sublet
and not so. cuts refashioned
concealed, roughed to face
anew. a new face
and name again, Joan Rivers
Molinsky. the battle-axe
and bawdy bitch. the brawler
and survivor and certainly
the funniest
the classiest
queen of the queens!
master of patter!
the re-formed rabbi of schtick!

gut-buckets in the corner
middle finger in the air

mean woman
you so mean   woman

the world
your fucking

living

room.

Nothing Sacred: Ode to Lenny Bruce

segregation is a dirty word
not *cocksucker.*

    loved in the jazz houses, the vaudeville mish-mosh dens for
    denizens
    the illegal sites of miscegenation

sucked cocks is beautiful
in the mouth
        better than
        bomb, vietnam
        than ahahahahahhahahahhahhah
        !!!!!

a whole life against the polite
of normal:

    kicked out of the navy for dressing as a woman
    dishonorably discharged for homosexuality.
    on the road as a kid in the thirties with comic
    ma, Sally Marr, divorced and running, threw
    Lenny onstage at a burlesque show, unannounced
    unprepared, after puking in the bathroom—he went
                              free!
    met his shiksa g-dess, Hot Honey Harlow
    in a baltimore diner over two eggs and bagel
    with marmalade.
                   broke his schtick then:
     the schmaltzy catskills impressions
     the corny jokes that killed and put him on tv

he really went for it, now
        man   on stage
        wanting to blow
        wanting to Bird
        Parker, pure mind
        and dirty veins
        mine everything
        in america, undo normal
        cut thru the bluster of stuffed jackets
        the pretension and phoniness, yeah!

                        Bruce
                        was a stage
                        name
        Leonard Alfred Schneider
        sounded too jewish like everything did
        the shy boy Lenny! alive under the spotlight
        of audience and a mother's love.

Lenny the Hustler!
        schlepping between shit houses
        working the craft. committed
Lenny the Moralist!
        refereeing what america says is right
        exposing the untrue, the not-good
Lenny the Rabbi!
        post-holocaust christian guilt and guilty
        the church is accountable, signed Morty
Lenny the old Schlep!
        bringing g-d to trial
        america in the courtroom
Lenny the Prophet!
        Elijah, opening doors

for exercising and excising freedom

all america is dirty
pure mind dirty
dirty mind pure

it all goes in the garbage
in the fuck-you bin
in the cock-sucking file
under frowned-upon
and fucked with

fuck you america
for killing lenny bruce
for untruing freedom
for the profanity you bomb the world with

Lenny the Alive!
Lenny the Saint!
jewish Lenny leading Yisrael!
        putting a cock in its ear
        a pussy in its heart
        to fuck itself

Lenny our David!
our junkie King!

Midrash of Roseanne Singing the National Anthem

Good Times for working white folks
in the late eighties. a chance to see
our overweight selves in the funhouse
mirror. the *domestic g-ddess*
as scrounger, scavenger
survivor despite reagan. baloney
scrambles and inventions
kinda like my mom
kinda familiar
this tv family
of workers. a marred
and rotating cast.

we were masks.

Roseanne knew that
early. her grandfather
chopped the name
Borisofsky to *Barr.*
her parents hid
their jewness
from neighbors in Utah
and passed in the mormon church.

marriage is a kind
of mask, like fame
and plastic surgery.
even name changes
can't cover up all
we are. empires
will crumble and sag

into the sea.
                                    i like to think
Roseanne knew this
in San Diego singing
the nation's anthem
in squeaked, shrieked tones.
on tv in a southern conservative
city near a giant military base
under the reign of bush I
on the cusp of war
she made a joke
a mock gesture
jester. a joke
on the empty
ritual, of thee
i sing, of heteronormativity
and militarism

this fat working-mom body
an easy punching bag on most days
grabbed her crotch and spit
a francis scott key dis track.
an antihero rocking
headlines and dumb pundit shows.
and to many of us
kids of the ninety-nine percent
whose moms Roseanne reminded us of sometimes
it became a triumph of sorts
of sports, this lady
telling the umpire
yelling the empire
belting a rallying cry
of calamity

pranking the WASPs
after a decade
of decadence
a dead audience
the goyim rattled
enraged.

& the fat
the working
the jews
who were still
jews doing their worst
to hide
this night
came out
their living
rooms and kitchen counters
with small propped tvs
in the dishwashing sections of diners
and late-night nurses' stations
the country over
rejoicing
or disgusted
had a laugh
a hardy-har
the night
Roseanne got the country
cracking
    up

WWLBD

i am backstage. one act in anarchy. a variety show
at the black orchid dinner theater. the fourth stage
in the second city. at this point in the evening i am wonder-
ing why i involve myself in such things. there is a juggler
here, i kid you not, a punchline plastic-chicken comedian
an improv troupe and a trio of sister hula-hoopers.
the audience is packed to the catskills. suburbanites
fresh off a bus for an evening of theater in the city.
my first set was a nice, easy round of nice jewish boy
who loves hip-hop poems, the humor and oddity.
i remind them of their son or their sister's son
the one with the drug problem. six hours earlier
my first book just cracked out of a cardboard box.
it is a book, yes, but it shimmered like diamonds
and i am supposed to be in the business of moving them.
the beginning of a long march to prove to my publisher
poetry sells.   and here i am.
two-fifty to three hundred in the audience.
i have them lapping words from my hand. words
that are poems. poems that are stories our people
have told since the Tigris.   but
it is months after the revisionist movie, months
into the second intifada . . .   and i am backstage
again, between sets, pacing. drinking water and bourbon
watching the improv troupe pander and schmaltz.
and i am stuck on obsessive repeat: *WWLBD?*
What Would Lenny Bruce Do? What Would Lenny Bruce Do?
and it's spinning like the slot machines they will play
at next week's outing and it's beating and hurting
my heart like some ancestral swell
my chest, a swill of drink. lifted head

false courage. terrified and could give a shit.
i am seventeen years old still fighting with teachers.
i am pre–bar mitzvah telling the rabbi to fuck himself.
i am poised and bombing. honest and iconoclastic.
there are stirs and gasps. murmurs and then boos
clinking tableware. loud voices beginning their rumble.
a white man stands and calls me a racist, others. other
things they say. i finish. the crowd, raucous and rabid
as i hit backstage, finish more drink, pause a moment
before walking out the wings, walking to the bar
in the back of the big room where the crowd is
now inconsolable. a man taps me on the shoulder
i turn ready to take a fist, he calls me an asshole.
he is removed by security. at the bar, there is a drink
waiting for me. the bartender is laughing. she is
Black and as beautiful as a James Brown song.

tuesdays with mel gibson

"When I was twelve, I went to hell for snuffin' Jesus."
Nasty Nas, on Main Source, *Live at the Barbeque*

old testament one-liner (a חי coup)

so yeah, i ahhh . . . invited mel gibson over to my house   to get stoned

passion of the kike

if you really want to talk about it
(and i think you don't)

let's start with your conquistador australian-aboriginal-killin
afrikaans-apartheid-separatist evangelical-klansmen crusade.

your alcoholic-rapist phallocentric lethal weapon
forced into temples of bubbes, abuelitas and granmammas
in every continent you ever got lost on.

you pompous pilate
roman-bathhouse-closing closet fascist, third reich–memorabilia-
collecting dick-sucker-like-Hoover damn cointelpro hollywood
mkkkarthy-blacklist Robeson jew-baiting pinko commie snitch.

you steadily been revising history
only got libeled kings' accounts of what happened
journals and gospels of war captains and capitalists
firsthand records lost like ashes in smoke-stacked ovens
indistinguishable like body parts in mass graves.

your church is full of shit
and martyrs beatified after you killed them.
this is not to mention Lumumba and Malcolm, Medgar and Emmett
the six million, gypsies and homosexuals, Galileo, all the strike leaders
Harolds and Hamptons, Lozanos you can't Lazarus. this is not to mention
crusades and inquisitions, missionary slave shackles with biblical
justifications american presidents enacting end-time scenarios with
the lives of poor kids sent to stand in front of missiles and die for the
cross (i mean flag).

you see stigmata so much
cuz there's more blood on your hands
than the hole of history.

i swear you can't read
ten commandments, first
being no G-d but G-d, and
you go makin him man.

Yeshua fought for the unheard
pointed to earth as kingdom, ripped crowns
until your pagan incestuous oligarchic divine-might ass
painted him blue eyes.

come on dude
you got the idea for your *nicht gut schmatte* of a movie
(and straight up i snuck into a sunday matinee)
from the visions of two nuns
nuttier than a Planters party pack
and seventy-two hours of gay porn.

Mary of Agreda
wore a blue cape around the convent
out her mind, imagined her body with spanish explorers
spreading small pox and vd in the new world.

Anne Catherine Emmerich's *The Dolorous Passion*
whose storyline you bit, mystically envisions jews
in hell for baking matzo with aryan blood.

in 1934 hitler applauded
the Oberammergau play
your movie's based on.

(this is what i'm tryin to tell ya mel)
your holy family has got more crackpots than a CIA cooking class.
your pops is a holocaust-denying zionist conspiracy theorist

but you love jews, you pray for us.
quick favor, save your prayers
shove them up your flat ass
go back to your cave in england
and *schtupp* all the cousins and sheep
your braveheart desires.

oh, you mad max?
you white-wigged patriot
raping slaves to prove what women want?

watch your back
cuz Danny Glover
lookin to play Nat Turner
next picture, Master Hawkins.

last thing before i finish
tapping this last nail
in your head—

give back my religion
cuz you fuckin it up.

nazi pope

truth is
his father was a german cop
and joseph ratzinger jr., the son
and pope, was a hitler
youth soldier who fought
with the ss. since his days
of armband and goose-stepping
he praised pope pius xii.
the pope who refused to denounce
fascists during the shoah. he lifted
the excommunication of bishop
richard williamson, a rabid
holocaust denier, and returned
to catholic mass a prayer
that asks g-d to deliver
jews from our darkness.

truth is
the pope is a nazi.
head of the largest house
of stolen bones. a museum
of conquest and coerced
conversions.

truth is
fathers carry bibles.
behind them
führers carry guns.

the pope is a nazi
and this is the truth.

henry ford wraps hitler's birthday present

You were a slave to that line.
You went to bed and dreamed about working.
You worked all night long
in your dreams.
Arthur Valenti, Ford employee, 1939–57

1

he actually ran out of paper
so ford went the route of absent dads on christmas
hastily remembered.

henry ford wrapped hitler's birthday present in newspaper.

newspapers he published, ironically.
the *dearborn independent*, folded awkwardly
over a piggy bank for hitler's fiftieth year.

the bow kinda brought it all together:
a red silk ribbon with a thick white stripe
strung thru its belly.

2

the union is run by jews.

3

ford employed overseers on the assembly line.
ex-cons and amateur boxers paid to punch
workers around. big men contracted to bully.

4

hitler had a portrait of henry ford framed on his desk.

5

henry ford is the only american named in *mein kampf.*

6

henry ford received the highest honor
nazi germany could award a foreigner:
the grand cross of the german eagle.

7

ford contracted with both the american
and german governments during WWII
making planes, jeeps, and other vehicles.

8

the model A
ford was a chariot
on a wooden plank
propelled by two bicycles.

the car, a way to separate
the individual from mass
transit, a solution to cavorting
with the funk of immigrants
and horses.

dislocated from the ground
the earth, one's own legs.
the body split in two
the torso rendered
useless. the body
obsolete.

9

henry ford published *the protocols of the learned elders of zion*
a conspiracy theory about jews running the banks and world
governments. this paper has been printed and translated and
used to rationalize despising and desecration and at times
destruction of a people.
                                    when in truth
henry ford sat on leather and ate stuffed geese during the depression.
henry ford garnered government contracts from all world powers.
his great-grandchildren eat well thru recession
and deindustrialization. they will never worry
or scour, cut coupons or go without a dentist.

10

the workers remain working.
the mind, a maze of worry.
dreams of work
of working
of holding
a job. the bosses
never worry.
they reign and rig
and reich
and wreak

havoc on the hands
of the callused.

they exchange pleasantries
on the golf course
chuckles in the boardroom.
they wrap each other birthday presents
in media owned
by ford
on empires
built
by fraud.

strange bedfellows: for american jews who no longer hyphenate their identity, vote republican, and think christians are down for the maintenance of our people

In the 38th chapter of Ezekiel, it says that the land of Israel will come under attack by the armies of the ungodly nations, and it says that Libya will be among them. Do you understand the significance of that? Libya has now gone communist, and that's a sign that the day of Armageddon isn't far off.
Ronald Reagan, 1971

They don't love the real Jewish people. They love us as characters in their story, in their play. . . . If you listen to the drama that they are describing, essentially it's a five-act play in which the Jews disappear in the fourth act.
Gershom Gorenberg on *60 Minutes*, 2009

the reason american christians
support israel
is to make us martyrs.

it says so in their book.
the one they stole from us.
the five of them really.

in order for apocalypse
manifest destiny in the muslin
cloth of nuclear holocaust

jews must be in israel
for the messiah to come.
not the messiah of equity

but a blond g-d, fireballs

in hand, jerry lee lewis mixed
with hacksaw jim dugan.

when he comes, in thunderbolt
tights and a diamond tiara,
we will be buried by rockets

and comets, and the great christians
will rise to heaven, or the space station
leaving us earth; a polluted war ball

everyone mad at us for not warning
the world when we saw reagan lean
into billy graham's hot, wet whispers

promoting the millennial plan, the promise
of eternity elsewhere, a ritz-carlton in the sky
a restricted country club in the afterlife

finally. the evangelical, ivy-educated, middle
american walmart shopper will have peace
away from our urban polyglot schmaltz stew.

somewhere far away, a perfect union like
the confederate south, an idyllic retreat center
with grass tennis courts and latin choirs

singing "g-d bless america" like Jesus
would, if he were christian
and white

Derrick Asks to See My Horns

Derrick was a thin boy
whose skin hung on him
like jell-o. acne, farmer's tan
dirt mustache, glasses, and b.o.
my roommate. freshman orientation.
southeast Ohio. he lived
near coal mines
and a couple of factories
that moved to somewhere
other poor people lived.

Derrick and i spent the night
on ideas, politics, religion, anything
free. holed up in a dorm
room on pell grants and a couple
of cokes from the cafeteria.

Derrick believed jesus was the savior.
Derrick never met any jews before.
Derrick thought jews killed jesus.
Derrick was told by his family and fathers
sitting on wooden pews in sunday schools
in the country's midsection
jews were the children of satan.

Derrick asked to see my horns.

it is 1993.

the drive from Chicago brought me
past gas stations selling fried chicken

tiny coops of white birds walking near the tumble
weed of frito-lay bags. all the green south of Columbus.

Derrick thought i came on a jack-ass pulled trolley
the red-star line, a dirty subway car, something
with wheels and borscht.

i thought he thought perhaps i played jazz.
Chicago-boy Benny Goodman, my quartet
would late-night the lone deli in Athens
Ohio. Zachary's, a New York yid transplant
where the three Black professors on campus
held court around bourbon to talk the night
to day.

i thought he thought i was a rabbi's son.
a shofar blower. announcer of days. usher
of the new year, ram horn trumpeter
blasting babylon awake in the year 57–something
or other.

or he didn't think
about jews or thought what he was told:
we were the wayward Judas, deicide
holocaust justified, devil kid christ killas
1-8-7 *on an undercover g-d.*

Derrick was dead
serious though when he asked
to see my horns.
zits like ripe cherries
crushed on his open face
sweet and stupid

with innocence.
sweaty in a bunked
room on the north green
in the cricket hum
of an august night.

Derrick's eyes magnified
behind his thick frames
when i pulled back the phantom
yarmulke i didn't wear

and showed him.

on the charge of deicide

I

i did not kill jesus.
jesus was a jew
and it's against the commandments
jewish commandments, btw
which jesus is, btw—
a jew. a dark hairy
semite who i am sure smelled
like some unscrubbable salt. i am certain
i did not kill him.
i wouldn't have
he was too down
at the time i was
too worried about some roman
governor's foot on my neck
or dick in my son.
i was too busy
paying some exorbitant tax
or hosting a secret meeting
to plot some sort of resistance
movement. jesus was participating in
some sort of jewish resistance btw
and i am for the resistance.

2

if your g-d's son were to descend
from another planet, some white-ass heaven
of burnt toast and chicken salad

if he were to walk on earth
and say a fucking thing
about an afterlife

i would gladly sharpen the flat edge
of a rock, the speared tip of a ram's horn
a broken bottle

i would love to shank your lord
and savior, except it's against the commandments
and i've heard what's supposed to happen next

and i would love to see your chariot come
and i would love to see you ascend elsewhere
and leave the earth to us mud people

3

jews did not kill jesus. maybe the nails and wood flanks were assembled
by some uncle tom/er, i mean there were jewish carpenters, after all.
but the erection of capital punishment is a state's declaration of
grandeur; such execution privileged expectation; the dream of men
certain of tomorrow;

the infallible decision
of empire.

The Centurion Classic

we were the jewish team / most of us anyway / me / the point guard /
the bench / not that there had to be a jewish team / but we were it / the
only one in the top 30 / (later that year we finished seventh in state) /
we'd been hearing about it since freshman year and never got an invite /
but since finishing in the top 16 last season / we were in / i guess they
don't count on that / having jews at the tournament / not that they would
with our impressive stable of NBA players / (Dolph Schayes anyone?)

the Centurion Classic was at a church somewhere downstate / some-
where with a lot of long john silvers / somewhere where strip malls are
battle-scarred parking lots in a lost american dream / where no one
quiet ever gets to the finish line / we got off the bus and walked into
the fieldhouse / two games ran simultaneously / shoes squeaked like a
nest of a hundred birds / layups and dunks and fast breaks / college
recruiters, parents, girlfriends, local newspapermen small-talked in the
stands / bodies rising, spinning off baselines, curling around picks,
sliding with the ball, denying, help-side D / three days of nonstop
high-school hoops / we ate at taco bell four times / met girls from St.
Rita's / none of us touched them / even though Millman said he did

it was spring / our small forward was playing baseball / our backup
center had mono / we played Westinghouse in the semifinals / Kiwane
Garris was the illest / second guard in state / Westinghouse was ranked
third / the game went into double overtime / we held Garris to four
points / in the first overtime Culhane, our four-man, fouled out / for
the rest of the game we played four on five / lost by three in overtime
number two

after the final game all the teams sat on folded chairs spread over the
two courts / the organizers thanked everyone for coming / sponsors,

coaches, parents, and the teams, for their sportsmanship / trophies / all-tournament team plaques / we came in third place after winning the consolation game / local politicians' and businessmen's speeches / a guidance counselor spoke about student-athletes / making sure to get good ACT scores for college eligibility

and then a priest took the podium / solemn and blond and collared like a penguin / and he asked how many of us accept Jesus Christ as our lord and savior? / ? / we thought it was a joke / i looked up and down our row like i was unsure whose name coach called into the game / he asked again in the negative / *how many of you do not accept Jesus Christ as your lord and savior?, raise your hand* / snickers, then silence / a fieldhouse of three hundred high-school boys and not a single word / hands began to dot the air / reluctant and few / a chorus of duck necks wilting / ashamed

but i answered the call / my hand shot skyward fighting for a rebound / A. J. hid his face in the round of his Cubs hat / Josh and Jason bit the lip of their jerseys to prevent their giggles from seeping into the makeshift pews / Rosenberg and Shapiro took their bags and sat on the bus / Hoff looked at me like i'd said i wanted to have sex with his cousin (which i did) / (want to) / the gentiles on the team encouraged me to put my hand down

two priests or fathers / or pastors / robed warlocks / came to get me / they asked if i'd go with them to what looked like the locker room / when we got there a couple of friars sat around like cops waiting for interrogation / bibles in hand / they asked what my name was / i told them Abraham / they asked if i knew jesus / i told them he was a Black cousin (like KRS had taught me) / they asked if i accepted him as my lord and savior / i told them i wouldn't violate the commandments / would worship no graven image displeased / the celibates were winding up / then the pitch / the passages / the fire and brimstone / the certain damnation / Luke and Matthew / finally the numbers i'd seen behind goal posts at football games / John 3:16 / came to life / the promise of eternity / three times they read the passage to me / slow and steady / as if giving directions on how to disassemble an explosive device / the consequences of my listening / dire

they read and reread about me burning / damnation for all eternity / i was seventeen and cocksure / and scared / i busted their full-court press like Isaiah / walked out the room / kicked over the grey plastic garbage can filled with gatorade cups and spit

tears damned
like prisoners

leather heart banging
against the wooden floorboards
in my chest

deicide

each winter a nativity scene appeared
in the center of old downtown northbrook
on a plot of land reserved for a flagpole
near a railroad x-ing. a plastic museum
lit all night. the immaculate birth
in a barn or something, in a town
of mostly jews. the night before x-mas
not a gentile was stirring
not even the cops. i stole the keys
to mom's '88 dodge convertible—
a car i learned to drive in and crash.
i rolled cold and layered
in the blanket of night, NWA
warming the factory speakers.
lights off, a boyz n the hood
drive-by kidnap of baby jesus.
his body frozen and hollow.
i threw him in the backseat
and drove to the football field
behind the high school, an abandoned
tundra. quiet wind and drifting snow
tornadoed around my ankles
like smoke. i walked alone
in the hour after midnight
arms at my side. in one hand the head
of jesus, in the other a screw gun . . . the 40
30, 20, 10 . . . i touched down
around his throat, held him to night
sky, back against the goal post
no one to witness, no one to save
him, william tell, metal thru his head
left for dead. i nailed
jesus to the cross.

the secret relationship between Blacks & jews

"Very few Americans, and very few Jews, have the courage to recognize that the America of which they dream and boast is not the America in which the Negro lives. It is a country which the Negro has never seen."
—James Baldwin,
"Negroes Are Anti-Semitic Because They're Anti-White,"
New York Times, April 9, 1967

The Indefensible Al Jolson

> *The entrance of the white man into jazz . . . did at least bring him*
> *much closer to the Negro.*
> **Amiri Baraka**

> *the misunderstood utterance of a prayer*
> **the opening placard of *The Jazz Singer***

this is our story.

the first sound ever heard from hollywood
an Africanized, jewish swing.
a bastard ballad.
a miscegenated song.

the second was Hebrew prayer.

the confusion here:
when the purchased
and purchasee cling
to what they are
relinquishing. the price
of the ticket can be reluctant
pain. the slow pull of a band-aid
or the slow push of a steak knife.

Al Jolson was Asa Yoelson.
his character Jack Robin, Jackie Rabinowitz.
his father wanted him to sing
in shul. Jackie/Al wanted to swing
in *New York, Broadway*
Home. Mother,[N] his own

[N] from *The Jazz Singer.*

147

didn't recognize him
blackened up, arms free
save the tear in his voice.
the tear at his chest.
his shadow self
exaggerating, accentuating
the music he loved
to steal. his face
changes when singing
this jazz. his body
enlivened. praising
his G-d. not just
mimicry, not quite
praise.

there is no rationalizing
his Plantation Act. fresh
out the cotton patch
in rags, overalls. a dixie
whistle in front of a slave
shack. where is the rage
the sharpening of blades
at least the dream of that
blood?   in 1927
what whiteman wasn't
racist. Debs, Dewey, maybe.
which one isn't now?

but in 1911 Jolson fought
to open the great white way.
cuz if you could make it there
you could make it
america. he helped

bring Cab Calloway
Louis Armstrong, Duke Ellington
Fats Waller into the prayer
book of american song. this instance
and incidence of solidarity.
he was the only whiteboy
allowed in Leroy's in Harlem
this is a badge and a charade
the world's greatest entertainer
took from the world's most pained.

his Mammy was Zion
and he was coming home
in the future, world
beyond, this time
he pleaded, wait for me
I'm comin'! Oh G-d
I hope I'm not late!
Look at me,
Don't you know me?
I'm your little baby![N] the confused
horrible hope of this new
country.

[N] "My Mammy," music by Walter Donaldson, lyrics by Joe Young and Sam M. Lewis.

on how jews became white

august in Springfield is without relief.
the lake a good five miles from town
an hour or more to walk. no cars or horse
to call yr own. those who live in the city
landlocked. hot. surrounded. pre–air conditioning
pre-meditated. the boyhood home
of abraham lincoln not emancipated
from the hate that made slavery.

for days white mobs roamed streets
destroying Black businesses, homes
bodies. the mob was working, poor
white. the wealthy far on the other side
of town beneath straw hats and moonshine
not lifting a finger, letting the heathens
fight it out for the city. the country-
side remained pastoral. this
the country's pastime.

> *(this vs., this pitting against, this grand-dragon stupidity
> of working white racism, this horror, this storming main
> streets to maim Black and Brown bodies who work for
> the same subsistence, this same pittance, never stepping
> foot into the boss's neighborhood, hanging those pristine
> white sheets out to dry.)*

at the center of this mob
abraham raymer, an odd-
jobs man. a worker, a theater
barker: convincing, conniving
knifing. a vegetable
delivery boy. weekly drop-offs
at homes of the well-to-dos. bunches
of kale, beets. heads of cabbage
carrots, ripe tomatoes.

what a job for a hebrew!
a peddler's son and a peddler himself.
leaving russia just changed the face
of the serviced, the fashion of petticoat
the currency of petty tips.
abraham would take it
until he couldn't.

> *(until he'd start believing the dream america tells its*
> *fair-skinned. the lie of pie, the destiny manifest, the lad-*
> *der built upward, n-word. the foot on and over the least,*
> *at least a constant rung beneath you, someone, some*
> *dung to look down upon)*

all the white heat went to abraham's head.
mid-august in the northern state. when the riots broke
abraham knew he needed an isaac. knew he needed
a knife. knew too well the elderly William Donnegan
he delivered vegetables to weekly
walking through the service entrance.
married to a white woman.   *(no mixing, america says)*
Donnegan, a retired shoemaker with a house
abraham didn't have.

(the stupid heat of august burning white grievance at
visible Black success)

there came a storm and beating.
abraham wielding a knife
the throat of William Donnegan
dragged from his home, in front of his wife
and neighbors. seventy-something years old

Donnegan is not isaac
Donnegan is the lamb
abraham sacrifices to the white
g-d of america

slit throat and strung up
front lawn of a house they'd burn
like temples.

abraham raymer
the yiddisher lyncher
the jury of peers
the acquitted
the freshly born
and baptized
american
white man

the white dream of irving berlin

irving berlin
taught himself
on piano
to only work
the black
keys

           are you fucking with us, izzy?

born israel baline
his earliest memory: his home
in ashes, the ransacking of cossacks.
father, a cantor (*of course*), real jazz
singer of the lower east side.
           izzy, the salesman

hawking newspapers on these streets
selling the grand lie in english
while his family humped in sweatshops.
this little news cappy who defined american culture
they say, the great white way.
of course he lifted the swing
of Alexander's ragtime
to create some hybrid, something more
something less. the g-d bless-
ing of america   *but which g-d izzy*
the masonic eye of the dollar
some betty grable in the sky, some Groucho
Marx/socialist jester
           are you fucking with us
                      izzy

this white christmas
this most a record ever sold
this song all the famous white c(r)ooners
slowed down and balled: bing, frank
the king, you are responsible
for these great grabbings

                              izzy!

what is it
about us that makes us
snatch and muscle?
                         this dream!

of white cold somewhere
in the desert, i get it   *izzy!*
this plea
looped nightmare
in heroic couplets
each december

              may all your christmases be white

you backed ike and war   *be white*
loved the shiksa   *be white*
heiress whose father forbade the marriage
                              be white
who you had to help in the depression
anyway
        may all your christmases

for you   *izzy*
                              what a dream!

154

a sauna of caviar
and mouth full
of shellfish.

the ashes of shtetl   *be white*
hawking street vendors   *be white*
the drunk insistence of rabbis   *be white*
and rats   *be white*
all that   *be white*

left
behind   *be white*
   be white
be white
   . . . *white*   . . . *white*
     . . . *white*
       . . . *white*
white.

blonde ambition

This was not a display of feminist power, this was the same
old phallic nonsense with white pussy at the center.
bell hooks, "Madonna: Plantation Mistress or Soul Sister?"

appropriates indiscriminately, criminally:
a red string, a red ribbon, robin, holy cow
batman! this taking (and faking) and profit
off prophets. bastardizing the Ballroom, a covert
convert. double agent cloaked in the cloak
of down. cloaked in an israeli flag in a city
with an Arabic name and brown roots.
a blonde girl's fucking Big Daddy Kane!
a blonde girl's fucking Big Daddy Kane!
a spectacle for record sales. this artifice.
art of fake in the shirley temple
Willi Ninja Bojangles. she got
booed offstage at the Garage.
xerox ain't real.   it is called pillaging.
this taking of Black babies, Black bodies
Malawi. the Black christ kissed on the cross
and brought off the auction block. a generation
demolished in the eighties, run over and renamed.
silence = death. you built a life on the dead and silent.
this is your religion, your occult, Mag   /sic.
this blonde ambition. this Black magic.

portrait with midrash of israel's favorite rapper

> *If I see a cop chasing someone down the street, odds are,*
> *you will see me running along to help out the cop.*
> **subliminal, israeli minstrel**

hat cocked in mimic. baggy jeans
some israeli team jersey two sizes too big
a costume after a Fu-Schnickens video.
a giant diamond-crusted star of david
hung on his neck everywhere he goes.

what privilege to parade
what was once hidden and stuffed
once branded on an armband
what a grotesque triumph
to emboss on one's neck.
how perfect—everything
stolen.

diamonds from south africa.
the adorned star perverted
by an imperialist state. the swastika
got corrupted at the ethnic cleaners

the star is no different.

his latest album is called *jew-niversal*[x]
c+c music factory meets a minstrel show
meets a zionist separatist rally. he starts
his concerts with a call to the audience

---

[x] i can't make this stuff up.

who's proud to be a zionist in the state of israel
put your hands in the air   hell, yeah

he is trying to make zionism chic.
literally paid by the government, a snitch
a just-say-no-to-drugs nancy reagan rapper
who is critical of young people resisting
military service. he takes a culture
that originated in a war zone
a nonviolent public performance
strategy, a future-world maker
& African Diaspora maintainer & elevator
and uses it to promote colonialism.
how perfect! this fat, wack nebbish
co-opts Black music to big-
up the zionist landlord.
how typical! historical
how unimaginative and jew-venile, ha!
how perfect! israel's favorite
rapper is a wack fraud
another jew in Blackface
a bastard(ization) of history
a tragic joke

how ashamed the elders must be

Avraham the Patriarch Was Black

this story is not mine
and is.
this midrash
this new talmud.

the rabbi said *impossible*
when i told him
what KRS-ONE told me
one night pressed against the face of Cory Anders's
boom box. he said it matter-of-factly
Abraham too was Black
on the sixth song of an album called *Ghetto Music:*
The Blueprint of Hip-Hop.

i was studying my bar(s)-
mitzvah. my welcome to the minyan
of men. the rabbi asked me to leave
right before i took the bema
he wanted to make sure i would never return.

so i wandered like KRS did Prospect Park
and men's shelters, some middle
passage between home and home-less
knowing the forever of being without ONE.

this is the man i've become
some wanderer, some Moses
some cypher conductor
trying to find a minyan
building new canons
new patterns & rhythms.

Scott La Rock is as much a father
as Abraham, but he too the body
Isaac, sacrificed for the g-d
of rap. KRS walked the earth
differently after Scott was gone.
s(w)ung intent/intense-ly
in the corner store of idols
a pentateuch of Lerone Bennett
Baraka, Howard Zinn, Madhubuti
and H. Rap Brown—smashing
and re-mixing, midrashing
the story to fit, to fact. revise
to re-vision as was, as is—this grand
gesture to proclaim, to pro/cure the truth

Abraham too was Black
which means he was also jewish
which means our father is the same
which means so many things
have gone terribly wrong

Ishmael, my love is some lonely place.
some messiah you choose to be.
you saved me, frankly
without wanting to
perhaps. and we don't believe
in saviors. but you raised me
right. turned this boychik
into a cock, full-grown wingspan
flipping the bird, flying
the coop, a giant coup
this song, this transmission
the reason for everything

i've ever done that hints at life
some eternal downness that pulls
my chest toward this truth:
my fathers are
have always been

two, Black

The Break (Ocean Hill–Brownsville 1968)

They will realize there is no way they can put a gag in the mouth of
Black people.
Leslie Campbell on WBAI radio, December 26, 1968

I

the what

in the six months after King was killed, the Bronx
and this section of Brooklyn stayed burning.

jews exodused to long island
while other parents moved in and remained
and wanted to make sure columbus stopped
lying and more than Crispus was mentioned.
called for decentralization & local school
council control.

the bosses and teachers' union agreed this time, for once, on something.
on september ninth, 1968, teachers went on strike.
Ocean Hill–Brownsville came into the crosshairs
of flight and re-population, center stage
in the empire state. jewish to Black
shtetl to ghetto, an american magic act.

the strike pushed the rest of the city like dominos
nine hundred schools closed for two months
thirty-nine class days missed
over a million kids
latch-keyed & plotted

the fear:
Black parents teaching Black
kids. Sonny Carson raising
a generation of nationalists

the teacher union
mostly white, jewish. scared by self-
determination. tragic irony. in the midst
of a war on other Brownsvilles, a nationalist
campaign of their own.

propaganda littered the papers
the head of the union, white/jewish
fabricated hysteria, a Black anti-semitism
he helped the media imagine criminalized
portraits of parental vigilantes
their militant children locking weak
well-meaning liberal jewish teachers
in their closets at knifepoint.

2

why local schools councils

ahmadinejad hebrew schools
josef mengele, the moil
frankenstein as an open-heart surgeon
john wayne instructing literature classes on Navajo reservations

at some point judas snitched cuz he was afraid of jesus's teachings

3

midrash

this is that moment of broken promise.
the choice to become fully white, here
for the first time in all eternity
the jew finally wore the mask
and full-body armor
of the whiteman.

for thirty-nine days
over a million children
walked around the city
in Indian summer
digging the fall
out. Big Daddy Kane
born a day into the strike.
Masta Ace two years into
the symphony of the Howard Houses.
kids wandered thru their parents' records
martial-arts film houses, endless train lines
seeking something to do

the white world abandoned them
the Black-jewish relationship ended

parents had to work and there wasn't
anyone around to hear them
to interrupt and alter and exploit
their first iterations, the children
alone for a decade to experiment.
hip-hop is born in this time

in rupture and fracture
utterance and gutter shit.

Flash cooking circuits
in his kitchen, self-
determined funk.
lord of the fly.

Public Enemy #1

In 1989 Professor Griff, Public Enemy's Minister of Information and leader of the Security of the First World, gave an interview to the Washington Times *in which he said that "Jews are responsible for the majority of the wickedness in the world." Days after the statement, PE's frontman, Chuck D, called a press conference.*

Chuck D sits in all Black
save the yellow stitched *P*
on his fitted cap. questions
float; ringlets waiting
for him to hang himself.

four days earlier elvis
costello slipped the n-word
through his thin lips. two
reporters were at the press conference

today there are fifty.
cameras like cannons
red light recorders armed
ready to shoot Chuck
dead in the canyon.

simple and plain:
Black music has a long list
of exploiters. middlemen
playing the role. a role assigned
by kings. The jew. The jew Jester
overseer, settler, seller of all things
Black, black-market bootlegs, money
laundry tailor-made, seller of all things
that may poison the king. it's precarious.

some of what Professor Griff said is true.
jew diamonds helped afrikaners. sold the raw
resources of the Black continent so long
they were afrikaners. this is wicked.
jews are culpable, creators of wickedness.

Chuck D bobbed and weaved a bit
then Ali-ed into the rope-a-dope.
all these white reporters and ADL
scriveners clamoring around his mouth
waiting like birds for some regurgitated
rant. lobbing explosives hoping to
retrieve the scrapped shrapnel like dogs.
he had them right where he wanted.
tired and panting, running for the story

Is Public Enemy Anti-Semitic?

eyes barely visible beneath his Black
brim. the twenty-nine-year-old avant-gardist
conjuring Fred Hampton and Aimé Césaire, fired
a shot they weren't ready for. a knockout
so quick you have to rewind it in slow-mo
to believe it ever happened. *The problem,*
he said, as reporters leaned in, warming
their faces in the fire, *is the system
of white world supremacy.* silence.
explosion. overpowering.
left hook. bomb dropped. he said

*i'ma leave it out
on that note.*

Louis Farrakhan Plays Felix Mendelssohn

Don't tell me that you understand until you hear the man.
Chuck D, "Don't Believe the Hype"

there is discipline here.

the Fruit of Islam scoured the auditorium for two days.

in april Winston-Salem is warm. white
and pink flowers bloom from dogwoods, a headdress
North Carolina will wear thru the downpour
until summer's blaze.

security detail so thorough they may have made the orchestral hall
the safest place in america.
                                 &
he may have given the order
to kill Malcolm
in a hot ballroom
in Harlem.

we may never know.
he may know and never say.

the program is called *Gateways: Classical Music and Black Musicians.*

in recent years the president of the ADL called him
the Black hitler. the white, jewish jazz critic
nat hentoff said the same.

skin complexion something light / Malcolm's
a history of mixing and terror.
tonight the violin is jammed

into his neck. his face hot
and inflamed against the brown
lacquered body of wood.

tonight Louis Farrakhan plays Felix Mendelssohn.
grandson of Moses Mendelssohn, the philosopher
who founded reform judaism. whose son
renounced the religion. converted to lutheranism
but Felix remained plagued by his jewishness
in germany. not until years after his death
did the world take notice of his genius.

the Fruit of Islam line the concert hall walls.

young men in suits and bowties
ready to die for what they believe.

there are more of them in hot wool suits
than there are members of the orchestra.

both groups in black.
both support the minister.

in response to the charge, he took the bait, said
hitler was a very great man. he wasn't great for me
as a Black man but he rose germany up from nothing.
there is a similarity, we are rising our people up from nothing
but don't compare me with your wicked killers.

Farrakhan is not responsible
for one dead jew. not one
left hanging
out to dry.
he is more gracious

with the bow, sawing
at the bridge, making four
strings sing imperfect fifths, plucking
life from jewish notes. he is making
music in this giant space
where there once was
silence.

the secret relationship between Blacks and jews

bizzy bone
david blaine
lenny kravitz
lisa bonet
their daughter
maya rudolph
sean paul
rain pryor
amiri baraka
 s kids
lani guinier
rebecca walker
rashida jones
slash
shyne
drake
abraham
jesus

&
you

don't stop
the body
rock

jewtown

in the fruit markets just west
my pops copped produce right off the truck.
he'd drop me & say to stay on halstead
between roosevelt & the viaduct.

i'd linger among pick-the-red-ball
shell-game hustlers, duffel-bag porno
salesmen who dabbled in colognes
socks & leather belts. on the south side
of the street a buffet of hubcaps, an open-
air department store for pimps & starter
jackets, a junkie yard w/ '88 special white rock
blankets of bootleg tapes, piles of plastic
bodies splayed like fallen dominos

Public Enemy records were four bucks
Cube's *Most Wanted* went for five
cuz record shops wdn't carry gangsters.

but jewtown wuz filled with gangsters
& shysters & hucksters & repo men

my grandfather knocked doors
from seven am seven days a week
demanding loot owed on layaway.
fur coats, suits, alligator shoes
leather couches, jewelry, & liquor.

jewtown was blues, then.
church folk & John Lee Hooker
amplified on sunday carts of metal.

white short sleeves & thin-black-tied
salesmen pushin Jesus & silverware.

by the time i got there
it was Africa. musk smudged
storefronts. beads & prayer rugs
Afro picks & posters of Malcolm
hung in natural light
like ducks & pigs in Chinatown

the one neighborhood
race mixing was allowed
the block spared from the great fire
where jim's original polish
piled fried onions & peppers
where blacks and jews came together
outside their homes to eat pork
and fuck white women
where muddy waters came
to plug in & make rock & roll

wholesale and ho sale
where cash was green
& rent was cheap
& jews were slumlords
cuz no one else wanted
to live there, a safe zone
even in the riots
& both daleys hated all
the mixing & tore it down
& paved it over

& now

there is a gold statue
a hawker frozen
a bluesman museumed
a caribou coffee

jewtown was a home away
from one, makeshift & janky.
a shtetl & ghetto & certainly
unjust it was, but it was
a home
north of the delta
west of the pogrom.

this was america   once
when blacks & jews roamed
on the holiest days off
to find a gun or girdle
some whitefish or pig's feet
in search of a deal or a scam
to get by & get over.

Don Rickles Roasts Sammy Davis Jr.

the room is mauve and mustard
orange and seventies maroon. fine
china and silver. crystal chandelier.
the head table is lined with celebrities;
Milton Berle next to Wilt Chamberlain.
it is 1975. the comedians and athletes
on the stage have brought their lives
of integration into public view. the jokes
are awful. *the nbc peacock is wearing
an afro.* Sammy in a tuxedo with gold
everything. big rings, golden shades
enough bracelets to adorn Kali.

this is a night of soul food and sour cream.
the boys and Phyllis Diller, backroom cut-up.
the Dean Martin Roast is a wreck. a peek
into life on the road, how funny people pass
time. insults and love punches that dance
the tightrope appropriate, that often fall
flat and quite uncomfortable.

there is none better and more horrible
than Mr. Warmth himself, Don Rickles
the last to roast. he is ruthless and wrong.
we need Blacks, he declares, a plea to america
pause and followed by a joke indefensible
out a whiteman's mouth. Sammy and Nipsey
Russell and Wilt and Dionne Warwick are all
crying now. Freddie Prinze Sr. is banging
the table and holding Sammy's hand.

the entertainers in america knew it
before anyone. they lived in the future.
the jazzmen sharing needles and reeds.
Cousy and Russell in Game 7, the same
stage. the same postwar, post-vaudeville
chit'lin slop chopped-liver circuit.
a love and trust in playing
together. a calendar of nights
grinding beneath stars that will fade.

they knew it
in variant keys
of horror. but they all knew
america was something
to laugh at.

something in which you could
perfect the gesture
and jester of public critique

i kid
    says Rickles
a bald and widening smart-ass.
wit dart sharp. sidekick and filler.
every punch lands perfect. set-up
side crack and open belly rumble.
we are brothers, he says, *we kiss, we hug*
Ric puts his mouth to Sammy's cheek
pulls back and asks the audience
                     any black on my lips?

talisman

Jesse is southern baptist hot
in a wide tie and three-piece.
natural, patted round as an eclipse.

this is cover   up for what he meant.

this is 1984.
cities are withering
there will be another eight years of republican white
house. bodies for prisons built for a private sector.
jobs shipped in boxcars overseas. the working
class sold back down and over the river.
the river is jordan. the only black man
the media will call highness
in this, his rookie season.

newspaper men say Jesse
called new york *hymietown*
the quote in full reads: *all hymies*
want to talk about is israel.
everytime you go to hymietown
that's all they want to talk about.

two years earlier Jesse was
keeping it real in polyester
and a clipped afro when he called
the israeli prime minister menachem begin
a terrorist.

this was 1982
there is a war in Lebanon

the Sabra and Shatila massacre
when the IDF allows the slaughter
of a thousand refugees.
jewish settlements growing
in Gaza and the West Bank.
state-sanctioned gentrification
by bulldozer and gunfire.
before the first Intifada.
before the shallow pact
broken in Geneva.
before crown heights
and after brownsville's
teacher strike. new york's
boroughs abandoned
like civil rights movement
offices. after the cross
bronx was built by moses.

in 1984 Jesse Jackson wins five
democratic primaries.
america is shocked. scared.
reagan runs for a second term.
the olympics summer in LA.
russians boycott. war-
heads stockpile.

while talking with milton coleman
of the *washington post*, Jesse asks
for a moment of realness outside
the glare of white lights.
Jesse leans and whispers in dialect
regionally specific to a decade
straight out of *Shaft*, any Blax-

plotation experience. milton
snitches to a white journalist
who goes on to win a pulitzer
who breaks the story all over
the morning page. which breaks
Jesse. the democratic party.

Jesse feels forces conspired
against him. forces that run
the media, that killed his King
campaign for president
forces that put him here
in a hot new hampshire synagogue
packed with tv cameras
and whitemen who own land.

Jesse is in a tallis
sweating beneath lights
in the temple. marked
by hearsay and sensation.
this is the night of his redaction.
tonight he is learning to white
out the truth
to cool fire
to expunge
flame.

the holocaust calls for its orthonym

i am box(car)ed. packaged and pimped.
hollywood (shockingly) doesn't tire
of making movies about me.
i am the h-card. h to the izzo.
you can run down my sleep-
over camps: dachau, buchenwald.
you know the bootstep and dollar
sign. can jigsaw a dinner set
dig the heil five and trimmed
facial hair, the striped threads
and multicolored armbands. you know
my biggest stars: orphan Anne
and schindler. of course the jew
spielberg had to let you know
there were some good germans.
you know all of this, you history
channel freak. you AMC WWII
easy to tell the good goy from bad—
type historian

but do you know
my original name:
my middle
passage

my ships and ocean
(blue) crossings. white
sharks and bones
at the bottom of seas.
white sheets and fruit
in trees. names forgotten

forever.
you know Primo Levi and Elie Wiesel
they are required in every high school:

but what of the Black anthem authors:
what of Ellison/Hughes/Hurston/Baldwin
Baraka/Walker/Cullen/Robeson/Lorde/Perdomo
Bonair-Agard/Pat Smith/Girmay/Brooks/& more

i am not american history's favorite subject
barely mentioned. it all
ends w/ lincoln. where is my link & lineage
my brand altered
at the altar
the bema
the church confessional

what photos of boats stuffed to the gills.
what body overboard hangs in your living room.
what land here stolen.
what reservations we have keeping natives alive
what Nakba and Maafa
what trail of tears and fire
what we must call ourselves forward.

know my name
say it over
the gaps
fill black   space
with Black
bodies. say it
again
until you get it

right
to learn my name
in total is to
(w)holy know your own

48-hour ars poetica

tonight
clouds traverse the sky
white soldiers occupying the deep
purple of the east: quick, silent. the giant
moon lights tiny bodies passing beneath.
on Eastwood Avenue trees canopy the street
quiet now after all the Mexicans, Arabs, and Koreans
closed the doors of their businesses on Kedzie Avenue.
the brown line starts to slow
at this hour in late summer. the air is cool
enough for slacks. i am wearing some
mauve polyester old-man pants
found in an arizona thrift shop.

yesterday
warm pink light
came thru the heavily sunned
drawn-curtained window of Aunt Estelle's
small bedroom. the light made me feel safe
and sad. Jules has been dead now
for some time. they lived here
in this modest four-room home
with a basement and backyard.
                          in Michigan City
where her father came to sell pants seventy years ago
where she raised a daughter who moved to montana
where one of her seven sisters lives not far, in a home
where most days memory slips her grasp.

i am noticing the light out the corner of my eye

Aunt Estelle will be ninety-two in december
is speaking of her father, in a small town in tennessee
during segregation. one of the two jewish families
in town, considered white until they said otherwise.

Blacks were forced to live on the outskirts
but on Saturday came to town
to shop and see a movie from the balcony.

whenever whites were on the sidewalk
Blacks had to walk in the street.

one day, my great-grandfather, David Schriber
a men's pants salesmen with the fortune
of seven girls, walked into the streets
with Black people and introduced himself
his family. this crazy little jewish man
shook a man's hand and said to him
we are the same
you & i.
when you see me
and my family, please
walk with us

it takes a *no*
then a series

a collection of new
imaginings

this is what i find beautiful
religious

this inch/itch
toward justice

these stories
i have to tell.

all the pharoahs must fall

self-hating jew™

on kedzie avenue and sunnyside
the barber's father brought his family
in '67. they left a land they called Palestine.
they were farmers there. and doctors.
the barber's son, a barber
plays opera. gives me a list
of poets i should read: Darwish
of course, Taha Muhammad Ali
Samih al-Qasim is a master
he says. and says the situation
at home is difficult, as he presses
a blade to my throat and separates
hair from the land of my skin.

the world, america, israel, jews
have separated this man
his family, all of kedzie avenue
north of montrose
from this land.
and i know its name
no one can tell me
otherwise.
it is called
Palestine.

™ As described by executives at HBO, right-wing bloggers, various family members,
and the national Hillel staff.

what it's like to be the disagreeable grandson of zionists

always after Patricia Smith

it's loud dinners and slammed doors. hoping
for an early death, a prayer for the cessation
of Palestinian suffering under your breath
after the hamotzi. it's more than four questions
on Pesach. it's republican dinner guests
with bad breath and bad jokes. it's knowing
they yearn for all-white everything. even the children
too olive, a goliath disappointment. not enough
doctors in the room. the stupidity of suburbia
and the indoctrination of watching tv and never
leaving the strip mall. it's people who believe
the world is flat and uncle sam's fairy tales
real. it's knowing we are not chosen
after all, we are just like any other white folk
who take what's not theirs and lie about it.

why i stopped going to shul

1

plush purple seats
high ceilings, stained
glass running the east
and west walls

white Abraham
white Moses
white David
colored like sheep
to look like everyone in the seats
below

2

the only memory i have from Hebrew day school:
Noah's ark wasn't big enough

3

in the lobby of Anshe Emet
around the corner from Aunt Joyce's house
where i'd stay when my parents worked
or dated, and for several years i went
for high holidays to break fast with her:
a mannequin models a bullet-
proof vest. computer printer laminated
paper taped on the wall explains:
in the new year, Anshe Emet
will buy vests for tortured israeli citizens.

please show your support for the victims.
write a check to. . .

4

the new rabbi
is new age-
y, only wants
congregants
practicing
yoga

5

on Kol Nidre
a representative from the israeli consulate
takes the bema, asked the congregation to support the wall
being built to protect jews from Arabs. a wall of hope
he calls it, to separate and secure. the rabbi is nodding.
the consulate representative describes how Palestinians
will not be able to enter Jerusalem, how there will be more
rigorous systems of checkpoints, how under our seats
lie envelopes, and how we can show our support this day.

6

the choir they rent
sound like goyim

7

the urban justice program

meaning the lone day we invite
Black folks to the synagogue
(minus those already employed as janitors)
is an MLK Day celebration
where we remind the Reverend's flock
that Abraham Joshua Heschel marched
with King   so it's all kosher

8

after Hebrew school
the parking lot fills
with BMW SUVs

9

during the ten days of Rosh Hashanah and Yom Kippur
we admit our transgressions; seek refuge in the forgiveness of G-d;
but first must receive the forgiveness of Others.

10

after the consulate representative speaks
Rabbi Siegel gives his sermon.
he praises israel
as the only democracy in the middle east.
weeps for the body count of jews living
the dream of nationalism.
he counts jewish bodies.
only our bodies count.
he recounts the call of the consulate representative.
calls for the maintenance of borders, checkpoints
the building of walls.

calls the knesset
the settlements
the united states
      just.
from the bema,
on the holiest night of our calendar
in the year 5764,
as the second Intifada is silenced
by missiles and war crimes
the rabbi is proclaiming G-d
's plan, and G-d's plan for israel
he says
like it was in egypt
is just
and must
be painted
with blood.

explaining myself

for my father

dad, don't be mad at me. this is not easy. i know what your friends
think: i want jews to have a safe place, of course. i want peace. you
always taught me to lead by example.   this time dad, we are on the
wrong side of history i mean jews who support israel without question,
i mean our family and friends in this country, i mean it's like we are
mississippi crackers, white south afrikaners when Mandela was locked
up. we are in the dugout pitching expletives at Jackie
Robinson.   history is repeating, dad, as it always does. in this
adaptation we are goliath, columbus. we dress in the whites of western
movies. the good guy wears white, is white,   but really is a killer of
natives. the ten-gallon stetson a southwest version of jim-crow
coneheads. our heroes don the cloak of colonialism, which is to say our
heroes take what does not belong to them in the first place, our heroes
say cool catchphrases, but these are the holy words of imperialists,
which is to say madmen, which is to say men who use bulldozers to
run over homes then build new ones, never acknowledging the horror
of what happened   the history just beneath our feet. dad, i am a
student of this country's history. i have been reading books, doing my
research every day since sophomore year of high school. any country
that receives as much military aid from the united states as israel does
must be up to some devious shit, must be going out their way to fuck
over poor people and people of color and more devious than
that.   there have been israeli lives lost. there has been retaliation in
the form of suicide bombs, there have been ignorant things said of
jews, in anger that rekindle our worst fears, but dad   very plainly
how many Palestinians do you know? when was the last time your friends
sat down and heard a first-person account of what happened in '48, in
'67?   *you* only have one side of the story   i have gotten the israeli
side, the american side, the columbus discovered a land without people

for a people without a land side   my whole life until i didn't. until i
decided to learn, to seek and sit and listen and know some of the many
stories. i am not the one who is turned off to listening   it is you
dad. you do not listen   your friends   this country   is not
listening you are too busy wrapping yourselves in flags of nostalgia.
ISRAEL IS NOT A DEMOCRACY.   how can it be?   was america
before Blacks demanded the right to be citizens?   was baseball
integrated before Jackie? wouldn't you say years later the national
pastime was racist?   this is history now, dad.   israel has all the
power, as does america, as do rich white people. Palestinians are
second-class citizens, at best   on land they have been on for
centuries.   they have to carry passports, their movement is restricted,
it can be impossible to go to your job or school to see cousins or the
doctor.   israelis run human beings off land, take land, i mean actually
take it. israelis bomb schools.   they do, dad.   israelis die too. but
they murder more than they die and if you were murdered i would go
after the people who did it, but   most Palestinians resist peacefully
every day. every day giant slights against them. human rights violations.
they are not free and you want all people to be free as i do,   as all
people who are kind and believe in equity and justice, but dad the
governments you support do not believe in these things, they do not
think all are equal, they think some are human and others are not. and
the others are people who are poor and of color and not backed by
billions of dollars in weaponry   this is real dad   this is the history
we will live   to regret.   dad   you are kinder than that   and
know better   we are better than this, we can turn the story right, work
together   with the many others to counter what is wrong.   i know
we can   you taught me to do this work, dad   and i believe you

Reflection on the Israeli Army Shutting Down the Palestine Festival of Literature in the Month of May in 2009: Burning Books, a Bebelplatz in Jerusalem

Where they burn books, they will, in the end, burn human beings too.

Heinrich Heine

jews love books.
we dress them up
in crowns and gold
breastplates. fine
paper, our finest
calligraphy. our books
live in an ark lit by a flame
that always burns, a metaphor
for a G-d we don't have
vowels for.

if we carry nothing
else into Diaspora, we carry
these stories, these scrolls
that unroll a history we revere
and parade thru aisles
on the highest of holy days.
we kiss the corner of tallis
to our lips, put cloth to text
to praise words Moses brought
off the mount, our ancestors
lugged thru the desert. stories
told and told again at a kitchen
table somewhere, the fifth and fifteenth
times we heard them bored out

our seder minds, but the fiftieth
and 502nd time something stuck
so we wrote them down
in our most reverent hand style
in the blackest of ink on bone
parchment. we record the trials
and rivals and lineage and heroes
of our families cuz we love books
mourn all the storied bodies
burned by the those who hate books
with messy endings. we love books
cuz books are bodies of stories
and stories make history
and we are a people who believe
in the stories of people to tell history
and mourn all the bodies and stories
burned before they are recorded
in the Eternal book, authored
by the voiceless and Vowelless.

but it is 2009/5769

& this spring israeli troops shut down the Palestine Festival of
Literature behind barrels of guns. they stormed into a theater where
poets were reading poems & demanded silence behind triggers where
bullets scream & governments checkpoint & knessets approve military
bombardments & schools are bombed & burned to the ground
they are meant to be on fire from words & ideas, not metal.

in the name of a jewish state
israeli-educated young men aimed guns in the faces of women
reading poems. in the name of a jewish state stories silence forever.

which raises the question(s):
who are we because of empire?
what democracy are we scared of?
how can we deny the right to sing, to *chazzan* a Palestinian song?

mad men bring books to the bonfire.
power-mad men bring bodies.

our books been banned & burned & bordered, bodied into boxes
& camps cuz they demand memory, insist our presence in the story
of the world & books are memory of never forgetting & people house
books in their stories & stories should never be crushed by missiles.
books record the day & days in exile & days that should not have been
recorded. the horrors & the horrible. the record of families split & bro-
ken & bastards forever. books are records that never forget & preserve
& serve memory & history when militarized revisers deny events as
lived by the natives. the records prove otherwise, proof of existence &
empires want proof of purchase & per chance & pursue silencing stories
that make them look criminal in the honest of day & moon of night.

records are stories, a people
hold dear. who knows this
more than us?

    all us   wandering immigrants
    all us   seekers of safe land
    all us   unfettered poets of wind
    all us   literate builders of pidgins
    all us   inventors with scraps
    all us   people of the book

        though we don't seem to know much
        anymore   except the havoc
        reaped on our bodies in exile, the learned

behavior of executioners we internalize
the bureaucracies & boots & lines of refugees
we terrorize. gather families into open-air
prisons & worse. we bury bodies in graves
of steel. bodies who house forests of stories.
where is the ark in the center of the congregation
the ark in the center of the city of peace filled
with bodies of stories, records stacked and unfurled
unsequestered & unsilenced.

it is mad men who burn books
& bodies & hold poets at gunpoint

this the work of emperors & empires.
furors & fascists. scared colonists
insane to control what no state could
the record of people living
despite the state's efforts
to have them not.

portrait of a slumlord

the slumlord is real.[$]

a short man pulls into the affordable-housing complex
his company built on greased government contracts.

rowhomes. nondescript. grey, cheap-looking. everything
in the area is tired. (except) the slumlord

drives a jew canoe, in the winter
wears fur. a diamond pinky ring.

the slumlord could be over-
taken by a pack of fat fifth-graders

but at the end of a chain-link leash
a german shepherd[!] named princess.

there is a small revolver in his waist belt
a sawed-off golf club beneath the driver's seat.

the money is green. the renter's Black.
the slumlord has a boat in Lake Winnipesaukee.

in a generation, the slumlord will not collect rent
himself. maybe send a son-in-law, a Mexican.

the slumlord gives to his synagogue, AIPAC, reagan's
second term, directly to the IDF. this isn't considered terror-

---

[$] Based on the stories told to me by my grandma's second husband.
[!] (Irony is lost on the slumlord).

ism. the slumlord hates Arabs, but has a Persian cat
who sits on his lap watching *law & order*.
the slumlord is napoleon short. the slumlord is my grandma's
second husband. she is said to have married well.

the slumlord is a stupid man no one wants
to sit next to at dinner. the slum is israel.

the slumlord is alive.

Now's the Time to Be Fresh

An ode to Students for Justice in Palestine's fourth annual Café Resistance

the room is so brown & olive
it scares people.
so smart & young it's illegal
to look this good: hijab & the out-the-box
nikes, kufis & hoodies, gold
& silver bangles make the body
a tambourine. heads nod
to Lupe/Kanye, indigenous Chicago
rappers who are Gon & Khaled.

eyes here, alert, trail into the corners
of faces like comets & my nose still
the biggest in the room
has healthy competition.

but the FBI doesn't like this room
and raided the sisters at four am
with subpoenas. tomorrow
the grand jury. they are organizers
graduating from college. in four years
a movement builds on campus.
students and administrators feel
this presence, this growing mass
who knows the hummus in the cafeteria
stinks and supports military brigades
& knows Finkelstein was denied
cuz of his commitment to rigor & truth.
this growing mass of Arab youth
who begin to ally with Black

student groups.
the campus an essential center
in pressuring America to divest
from South African apartheid.
Kadeem Hardison & Laurence Fishburne
in Spike's *School Daze* kind of freshness

the culture's multi-ethnic
the room electric.
now's the time
end apartheid in Palestine!

shiksa angel

an ode to Rachel Corrie

oh Rachel Corrie, shiksa
gone mad. angel standing
before bulldozers, arms spread
welcoming a raging star. white
and blonde and sun-kissed before
a home the government is trying
to rubble. immovable Venus
stoic goddess, the heroine
in our hearts.

your parents fight in your name.
your letters are read as prophecies.
you are considered a martyr, a model
of solidarity. i hope there is youtube
in heaven and you watch your picture
raised at protests, hear the cantata sung
in your blues. your play travels
across country to educate the regular body
to stand and ally and outrage at injustice.
i hope there is fattoush and fatwa
where you are, a mirror to see
your beautiful ghost.

all the pharaohs must fall

Mohamed Bouazizi didn't have a permit to sell fruit
didn't have government permission to earn a living
to live. the police took his fruit and slapped his face
he went to the governor's office. they refused to see him
he poured paint thinner on his body
        and lit the match

all the pharaohs must fall

we needed inspiration, to be awakened
in our bodies, our lives made present
here we are
the world is not right, just, or fair
the most have the least
the least have the most

all the pharaohs must fall

all the kings of jordan
all the queens of england
all the bridges crumbling
dictators like dominos
israel is a pharaoh
and must fall. all the leaders
with colonial control
who ransack resources
in Africa, who steal
lives in East Oakland
who protect jon burge

all the pharaohs must fall

all the pharaohs who reign
over fruit sellers and farmers
the world over
the world is over

all the pharaohs must fall

the tycoons and filthy rich
heads of state on the chopping block
chairmen ousted from their seats.
there are many ways to do this
the giant is waking, it is the body
of the people who have little
to fall back on. no doctor or bank
account. the people who hand to mouth
who check to check. all this
scrounging kept us occupied.
all the gathering of crumbs
left us looking at the ground
but the bodies ablaze have given
us literal whitmans, at wit's end
they sing the body electrocuted
incinerated, sparks to wake us in the war machine
wake us in the mineshaft stuffing rich men's pockets
wake us in our second jobs, our second mortgages, our second marriages
wake us in the routinized mechanics of our own labor
wake us cleaning gold toilet bowls, searing foie gras
all security guards, fast food line cooks and cashiers
all barbers and teachers, basket weavers and tea makers
all field hands and construction workers
all women with needles and men with hammers
all bodies who drive or lift, who sweep or cook
everybody who takes away, who takes orders

everybody whose body needs a break or bus pass
who needs an eye exam or job or a better job
everybody whose body is uninsured, underfed
unaccounted for by governments and corporations
who bureaucratize their love

wake in this new day
look around
neighbors are allies
we don't have to compete with
we can ally and fight with them
there are more of us
who don't drill or bomb or legislate
more of us who third-shift and wash dishes
more of us who forge papers and sneak over fences
more of us worried about unlawful arrests
and whose worry arrests in the night without sleep

wake in this new day
we will all die soon
let us live while we have the chance
while we have this day
to build and plot and devise
to create and make the world
just
this time for us
this time for all
this time the pharaohs must fall

what will i tell my jewish kids

after Dr. Margaret Burroughs

who may not really know they are.
whose parents eat BLTs in the country
club and practice capitalism on the Sabbath.
whose suburb began voting conservative
in the generation after civil rights
whose great-grandfathers survived the shoah
and whose grandfathers suffer Islamophobia.

what will i say to my little nieces and nephews
who celebrate christ's mass, who hunt for easter
eggs, who like mel gibson movies, who adore
the whitewash and wonder bread on pesach.
what will i tell my little homies who run out of gym
class asking why their cocks are cut, what will i say
when the girls' noses grow, hair frizzes, hips widen
when they don't look a damn thing like barbie.

what do i tell the bar-mitzvah boys who end up studying
man's law before G-d's. what will they understand
of pigeonholes in a pidgin their tongue has no taste for.
i will tell them: we are middlemen, liminal women, go-betweens
seams in babylon, alephs holding the sky and earth
together, synthesizers of the sacred and profane

we are bankers. pagans and christians thought it devils' work
and we wanted to survive, so we are hustlers, pawnbrokers
slumlords. the white folk who lived near Black folk. of course
we got into the music business, the exploitation. we love
the blues, the melancholy melodies remind us of our own

chazzan. our own sorrow and diaspora. we George Gershwin-ed.
we blackened up. we wronged our neighbors. we connect a country
always on the brink of civil war.

we are a bridge people. red sea parters. translators
between the warring. we see connections. the i in i
the i in thou. Buber taught us that or was it Haile Selassie
or Freud? and what was it Marx demanded, we live as Moses
bent and davening toward justice. a radical equity where everything is
sacred or nothing is. Einstein to unify the chaos.
Emma Goldman to arrange the pieces.

i will certainly tell my jewish kids
of Goodman and Schwerner who died
with their brother James Earl Chaney.
that for a time, we were freedom riders
along with others, we were central
in the movement. hated jim crow
ourselves, for a time in this country
we were the Others, now we are other
than our selves.

i will tell my jewish kids
we have a long story. more than what is seen
now. we are a people who wander and wonder
who have a bag prepared in the corner. i will
tell them israel is not a jewish state. it is
an empire state, a state against people
and a state against G-d. a G-d who is
borderless and nationless, a G-d who is
certainly without drone missiles and air
raids. in a jewish state no tank stands
between people seeking water or medicine.

israel is a farce, the guilt of the western world.
a christian admission of the holocaust.
a watchdog over oil. a stepchild power mad.
a baby country raging against everything
i know to be jewish. i will tell them, help dis-
mantle israel. Zion is yet to be, it is in the struggle
of becoming. this is the truth. it will venerate us
it will exodus, the truth will set us free!

post-schtick

post-schtick

Seven Israeli teenagers were in custody. . . . witnesses described
an attempted lynching of Palestinian youths.
New York Times, August 21, 2012

1

after the ha-ha
bombs drop on Gaza

a ghetto
a shtetl

bombs that bear autumn's scent and winter's chill.
bombs that batter. bombs that kill.[א]

2

we did not come to this country
to become whitemen

but we have become
white.men

blindly telling
the tired tale of columbus.

we learned so much
from our executioners

[א] Lara Aburamadan, "Trapped in Gaza," *New York Times*, November 16, 2012.

we became
executioners.

3

bolsheviks became stalinists

4

we who were routed into work camps & gas chambers
now fence bodies into concrete graves.

5

let's call it what it is:

apartheid. genocide.
give it

a proper name
an orthonym.

6

you don't ask the mouth
from which the rope hangs
to explain the reasons
it's being lynched

you grab the hands
that fashion the noose
&
break them.

baruch Hashem.

Acknowledgments

shouts:

to Roger Bonair-Agard who ordered & edited this *Schtick*

to my peoples Idris Goodwin, Adam Mansbach, Angel Nafis

to Young Chicago Authors staff & teaching artist corps

to all Louder Than a Bomb poets for their courage to truth

to Anthony Arnove, Julie Fain, & the Haymarket Books massive

to Sarah Grey and Dao X. Tran on the edits

to Brett Neiman for killing the design

to Saba of Pivot for the tracks we making for the *Schtick* EP

to Danny, my pops—the G.O.A.T. of storytelling

to Susan, my moms, my heart & fire

to my brother Eric, Elyse, Addison, & Colin, i love all y'all

& to Sarah Macaraeg, whose courage & consistent realness make
    me want to write more & better. i love u.

& for you, reading now. my gratitude. my gratefulness.
for real.

About the Author

KEVIN COVAL is the author of four poetry collections and two chap-books, including the American Library Association Book of the Year fi-nalist *Slingshots: A Hip-Hop Poetica* and, most recently, *L-vis Lives! Racemusic Poems*, described as a "stunning, and very personal, piece of literary work that should be required reading in every high school in America" by *Impose* magazine. He is a native of Chicago.

Coval founded "Louder Than a Bomb: The Chicago Youth Poetry Festival," now one of the largest youth gatherings on the planet, recently the subject of an award-winning documentary of the same name. Coval currently serves as artistic director of Young Chicago Authors, the non-profit home of Louder Than a Bomb. He teaches at the School of the Art Institute of Chicago and is a frequent contributor to WBEZ Chicago Public Radio. @kevincoval